faThGirLz!

BIG BOOK OF
QUIZZES

FUN, QUIRKY QUESTIONS FOR YOU AND YOUR FRIENDS

From the Editors of Faithgirlz!

Other books in the growing Faithgirlz!™ library

NONFICTION

Best Party Book Ever!
From invites to overnights and everything in between

Faithgirlz! Handbook
Faithgirlz! Journal
Food, Faith and Fun, Faithgirlz! Cookbook

Girl Politics
Everybody Tells Me to be Myself But I Don't Know Who I Am
You! A Christian Girl's Guide to Growing Up

DEVOTIONALS
Finding God In Tough Times
No Boys Allowed
What's a Girl to Do?
Girlz Rock
Chick Chat
Real Girls of the Bible
My Beautiful Daughter
Whatever!

BIBLES
NIV Faithgirlz! Bible
NIV Faithgirlz! Backpack Bible

BIBLE STUDIES
Secret Power of Love
Secret Power of Joy
Secret Power of Goodness
Secret Power of Grace

FICTION

The Samantha Sanderson Series
Samantha Sanderson at the Movies (Book One)
Samantha Sanderson on the Scene (Book Two)

The Good News Shoes
Riley Mae and the Rock Shocker Trek (Book One)
Riley Mae and the Ready Eddy Rapids (Book Two)
Riley Mae and the Sole Fire Safari (Book Three)

From Sadie's Sketchbook
Shades of Truth (Book One)
Flickering Hope (Book Two)
Waves of Light (Book Three)
Brilliant Hues (Book Four)

The Girls of Harbor View
Girl Power
Take Charge
Raising Faith
Secret Admirer

Boarding School Mysteries
Vanished (Book One)
Betrayed (Book Two)
Burned (Book Three)
Poisoned (Book Four)

Check out www.faithgirlz.com

Big Book of Quizzes
Copyright © 2014 Red Engine LLC, Baltimore, MD

Requests for information should be addressed to:
Zonderkidz, 3900 Sparks Drive SE, Grand Rapids, Michigan 49546

ISBN 978-0-310-74604-1

Done in association with Red Engine, LLC, Baltimore, MD

Zonderkidz is a trademark of Zondervan.

Editors: Kim Childress and Karen Bokram
Contributors: Katie Abbondanza, Kristi Collier Thompson
Cover and interior design: Chun Kim

Printed in China
14 15 16 17 18 19 20 /DSC/ 10 9 8 7 6 5 4 3 2 1

CHAPTER 1

All About You

CHAPTER 2

School Sitches and Stuff

CHAPTER 3

Besties, Boys and Other Bafflers

CHAPTER 4

Faith and Family

Hey, Faithgirlz!, welcome to the wide world of, well, you! This awesome cool collection of quizzes lets you delve into everything from faith and family to besties and boys—plus everything in between.

These questions will have you examining just about every part of your life. You'll discover new things about yourself, your crew, crush, parents—stuff that's never even dawned on you before. More than 20 quizzes are broken up into four neat little categories: All About You; School Sitches and Stuff; Besties, Boys and Other Bafflers; and Faith and Family.

Just grab a pencil and maybe a pal, and flip through. And now your very first question: Are you ready for some quiz-tastic fun?
Thought so!

– the editors

CHAPTER 1

All About You

Maybe it seems funny to take a quiz about yourself. Shouldn't you already know everything? You are you, after all. But you might not know *everything*...

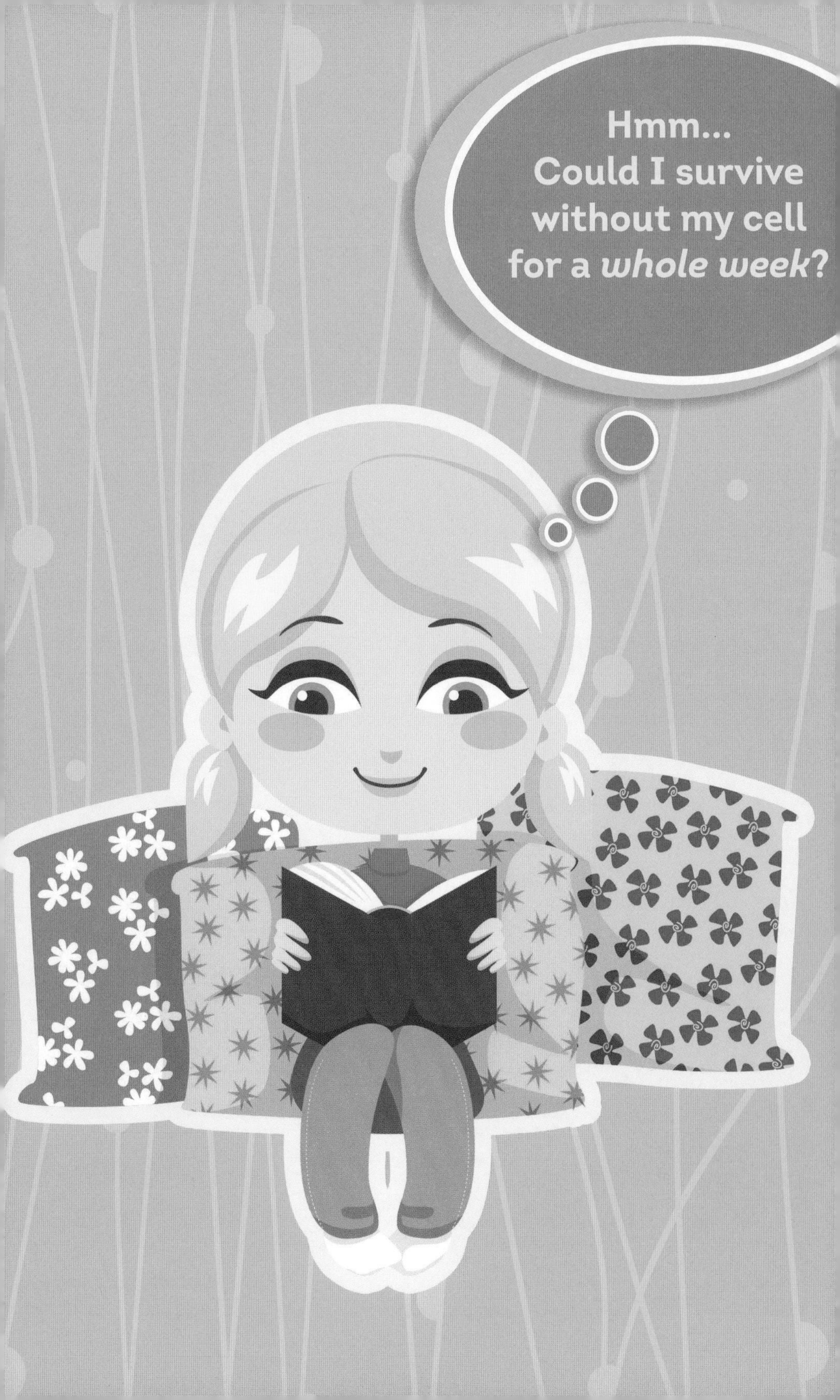
Hmm...
Could I survive
without my cell
for a *whole week*?

Circle all the words that best describe you. Choose as many as you like—this special combo is all about your amazing personality. Chances are you and your friends will have different picks, so have fun comparing notes.

Graceful

Fun

Energetic

Honest

Quirky

Flexible

Creative

Dramatic

Messy

Loyal

Adventurous

Personality

ARTISTIC

Sensitive

Friendly

Clever

Caring

Calm

Organized

Helpful

BOLD

Quiet

Sweet

Athletic

Studious

STRONG

Witty

Musical

Are You Cool

Life is filled with so many twists and turns, it can almost make your head spin. Or not, if you're a go-with-the-flow girl. So, are you ready to face the challenge of change? Find out.

 Your mom's new job means a major move to another state. Are you psyched about your first day at a fresh school, mid-year?

A. Big-time! You're always up for an adventure.

B. Psyched? Try terrified. You have no clue how to dress, act or even breathe.

C. A little bit—you're trying to be flexible. You've decided you'll just be yourself and see what the kids and teachers are like.

 You were stoked to make the basketball dance team, but right before the season is supposed to start, you find out the squad's been axed due to budget cuts. How do you deal?

A. You go into the mega-pout of all time and refuse to even consider a new activity. You wanted to cheer—end of story.

B. You shrug it off. Sure, it's a bummer, but hey, now you'll have time for guitar lessons.

C. You ask your coach if you and your friends could raise cash for the squad on your own—maybe by hosting a bake sale.

3 Your parents tell you they're adopting a baby girl. What's your biggest concern?

A. You're so busy, you won't be able to spend enough time with your new little sis.

B. They'll get so intense about the baby that they'll totally forget you're alive.

C. You might lose a few zzz's if the baby cries at night, but you'll roll with things as they happen.

4 You've been beyond looking forward to hitting the slopes with your BFF's family. But on Thursday, you come down with a gruesome case of the flu. Ick. Should you suck it up and still head to the mountains?

A. Nope, that's selfish—no need to spread the misery.

B. Sure—the cold mountain air might bring down your 102 degree fever.

C. You'll see how it goes—if you wake up in the morning and still feel sick, you'll take a pass.

5 Yay, sleepover! You're all watching your fave movie when Maddie suddenly screams, "Enough! Let's do makeovers." Are you into it?

A. Kinda-sorta. You're not super into makeup, but you can always wash your face when you get home.

B. Yes, indeedy. You love trying out new looks, even when they're a bit bizarre.

C. No way. Maddie's known for her fascination with blue eye shadow. You pretend to instantly fall asleep.

You aced your audition for *Alice in Wonderland*, and you're sure your drama teacher will cast you as Alice herself. When you stop trying on gingham dresses long enough to check the final cast list...it turns out you're the mouse. Your reaction?

A. You stomp off to find your teacher and tell her you're quitting the play altogether.

B. You shake off that disappointment. Even with a small part, you can still have a total blast.

C. You vow to become even better by learning all you can in this show about singing and dancing. If you work hard enough, next time you'll snag the lead.

You think your friend's birthday party is going to be at the bowling alley, but a last minute change of plans means you're heading to a rock climbing gym. You...

A. Tell your friends you twisted your ankle and sneak out of there. There's no way you'll have fun trying to crawl up a wall for an hour.

B. Throw caution to the wind and start climbing. It may not be your thing, but you might as well try to have a blast (and who cares if you look silly?!).

C. Admit your lack of skill and stick close to a nimble friend—you cheer her on as she heads up the face.

You go over to a new friend's house for dinner. She's from South America and eats food that doesn't look like anything you've ever tried before—and you're pretty sure you can see an eyeball. What do you do?

A. Take a deep breath, pick up your fork and give it a try. There are plenty of dipping sauces to cover the taste and, hey, maybe it won't be that bad if you can just stay away from that eyeball...

B. Stuff the whole thing in your mouth, eyeball and all. Hopefully, everyone watching will be impressed.

C. You refuse to take a bite. From the looks of it, that thing is practically still alive!

You've been saving up for some amazing new shoes, but then you accidentally lose your phone—and this time it's coming out of your allowance. Now you're back at square one. You...

A. Give up on the shoes. So adorable, so not meant to be.

B. Let out a big sigh, then buckle down and pass out flyers around your neighborhood advertising your mad lawn mowing and babysitting skills. You're determined to have it all.

C. Go straight to your mom and beg her to give you the money you just lost on the phone. Hopefully, she'll take pity on you and hand over enough cash for those kicks.

Your English grades are so sky-high your teacher recommends you switch to a super tough honors class next term. Do you make the move?

A. You'll give it a trial period. If you get in over your head, you can always switch back.

B. Of course—you're so up for the challenge. Besides, she wouldn't suggest it unless she thought you could really handle the challenge.

C. Nope, you're staying put. What's the point in taking on harder work?

Flip the page to find your answers (and how to deal!).

Add up your points to see where you fall on the change-o-meter...

	A	B	C
1.	A. 3	B. 1	C. 2
2.	A. 1	B. 3	C. 2
3.	A. 2	B. 1	C. 3
4.	A. 1	B. 2	C. 3
5.	A. 2	B. 3	C. 1
6.	A. 3	B. 2	C. 1
7.	A. 1	B. 3	C. 2
8.	A. 2	B. 3	C. 1
9.	A. 3	B. 2	C. 1
10.	A. 2	B. 3	C. 1

24-30 POINTS: CHAMELEON CHICA

You're the kind of girl who thrives on change—it makes life fun, fab and fascinating. You keep a positive attitude when unexpected problems crop up. If life hands you lemons, you start setting up that lemonade stand. Just remember to keep a few things in mind. One, don't let that sense of self-assurance make you take unnecessary risks that could lead you off track. Just because an opportunity comes up out of nowhere, doesn't mean you have to face it full-throttle. There's nothing wrong with a healthy dose of caution. And two, don't be so willing to change that you forget who you are deep down inside. Always listen to your gut and the power of the Holy Spirit—they're gonna guide you and keep you true-blue to your values and beliefs—always.

17-23 POINTS: CAUTIOUS CRUISER

You totally get the fact that nothing stays the same, but you like to take your own sweet time dealing with those inevitable changes. One of your best qualities is the way you think out a situation from top to bottom before you commit to action. Not only does this prevent you from making quick-fire mistakes, it gives you the time you crave to get used to changes we all have to face. Your balanced approach is totally awesome. You understand in your heart what the Bible means when it says in Ecclesiastes 3:1, "There is a time for everything, and a season for every activity under the heavens."

10-16 POINTS: QUEEN OF CONTROL

Safe and familiar scenarios are your comfort zone, and you don't wanna leave any time soon. It's understandable to want to control what happens to you, and it's normal to freak out a little at the unknown—which is what makes change so scary sometimes. The trick is to stay in trust and faith no matter how things might appear to you. So, what's your game plan? Try this: Make a list of five times in your life that you faced the unfamiliar, and it paid off. Could be the inaugural time you tried sushi—you were scared to take a bite, but now it's your fave. Could be the day you held your breath and swam underwater for the first time—that led to your success today on the swim team. Push past the fear by telling yourself the payoff could be amazing. God's got your back, promise.

We all deal with a bazillion choices on the daily. Do you agonize over every outcome or make your selection in a snap? Reveal whether you can make the perfect pick or end up fretting forever.

The pricey cross-body bag you've been eyeing for months is finally on sale. Problem is, the only purse left is in a not-so-sunny pea green. You...

A. Gleefully plunk down your cash. You're positive you can make it look amazing, despite the color. And don't you have a green scarf somewhere?

B. Snap a pic and post on Instagram to see how many likes you can rack up, all while guarding the kinda-sorta dream bag with your life.

C. Snap a pic and send it to your bestie. She knows your closet even better than you.

Your older sis is stuck between two great guys to ask to the upcoming Snow Ball. When she comes to you for advice on whom she should pick, you...

A. Sympathize, but tell her it's ultimately her decision, and she should give it lots of careful thought.

B. Choose the cuter one. Really, what else is there to think about?

C. Grab a pen and paper and help her make a list of pros and cons. It works for you every time.

Your Mind?

The girl you sit next to in math just sent you an evite to one of her infamous bashes this weekend. You...

A. Check your schedule to see if you have any previous plans. You don't want to double-book. Eek!

B. Peek at the guest list before sending an RSVP. You'll only go if your friends are going, too.

C. Shoot an instant "yes" and plan your partywear. You've been dying for an invite all year.

Woo-hoo! It's taco day in the caf. But just as you're about to ask for two, *por favor*, the lunch lady brings out a bubbly hot slice o' pizza. You go for...

A. Neither. At least not yet. Instead, you hightail it to the back of the line to give yourself more time to figure out this midday humdinger.

B. Your first pick, and you have yourself a fiesta. You can have pizza another day.

C. Both. Sure, you might get a serious case of food coma by fifth period, but it'll be worth it.

You and your BGF Michael have always had a blast hanging out, but lately he's been blowing you off and you're not exactly sure why. How do you deal?

A. Confront him and ask what's up.

B. Spend extra time with your girlfriends. Sometimes guys just need a li'l space, right?

C. Ignore it. Could just be a phase.

6 You're getting an award at your school's assembly, and you're all set to wear your new spring dress. But when you wake up, the weather's 30 degrees colder than it should be. You...

A. Throw your puffy parka on over the dress. It'll be warmer inside, right?

B. Default to one of your go-to winter outfits. Alas, your fabulous new frock will have to wait for warmer weather. Darn that polar vortex!

C. Freak out while you dig through bins of stowed-away winter clothes. Ugh! You're gonna need a whole new outfit concept.

7 Your Bio teacher is offering 20 extra-credit points to anyone who volunteers to help her set up the science fair after school today. You could definitely use the boost, but you have tennis tryouts. You...

A. Dial up Mom to see what she thinks. After all, she's the one who really cares most about your grades.

B. Go to tryouts, duh! You're fairly sure you're destined for Wimbledon.

C. Ask your teacher if you can skip out early and snag just half the credits. It's better than nothing.

8 In an amazing stroke of luck, your grandma pops by on your birthday and grants you one present of your choice—sky's the limit (well, almost). You...

A. Debate between the trendy boots you've been eyeing for weeks and some practical sneaks. Your kicks are totally trashed, and you need a new pair ASAP.

B. Immediately ask Grams for an iPad mini, please and thank you.

C. Say you'll get back to her. It's such a surprise, you totally can't think straight when put on the spot.

Add up your points to see if you can make up your mind...

1.	A. 3	B. 1	C. 2
2.	A. 1	B. 3	C. 2
3.	A. 2	B. 1	C. 3
4.	A. 1	B. 2	C. 3
5.	A. 2	B. 3	C. 1
6.	A. 3	B. 2	C. 1
7.	A. 1	B. 3	C. 2
8.	A. 2	B. 3	C. 1

8-13 POINTS: NAIL BITER

You're slow to make decisions—but that's not such a bad thing, is it? Some people need more time than others to mull things over. Sometimes when you take it slow, you end up making better choices. But don't let your fear of choosing the wrong thing keep you from enjoying life in the moment. You make a lot of little decisions every day that aren't worth fretting over. And if you really get stuck, you can always turn to God. No question is too big or too small for him, and he has all the answers. So ask away!

14-19 POINTS: **STEADY BETTY**

You've got a level-headed approach to navigating your way through tough situations. You have no problem asking others for advice if you need it, but you can also rely on your intuition to draw your own conclusions. Keep up your sensible approach to decision-making and you'll be able to overcome every challenge that's put before you. Remember to add a splash of spontaneity to your life once in a while—sometimes, being impractical can be fun.

20-24 POINTS: **SNAPPY SISTER**

Whoa, speed racer, there's no decision too difficult for you. You know what you want pretty quickly—and you're usually confident in your choices. It's great that you're able to go with your gut instinct, but sometimes making hasty decisions isn't the best approach. Certain issues need to be looked at from all angles, and taking the time to noodle those major choices is necessary. Bouncing big decisions off a BFF or your parents can help. Still feel stumped? Talk to God about it. He's always listening.

Are You in a Rush to Grow Up?

Your days of playing with baby dolls and doodling in coloring books are pretty much behind ya, right? Well...it depends. Some girls are so past the kid stuff, while others can still be found munching on Pop-Tarts and sneaking in Saturday a.m. cartoon sessions on the regular. So where do you fall on the rush-to-grow-up scale? Find out...

Your mom is spring cleaning, and she's insisting your room be de-cluttered. When she starts by tossing some stuffed animals in a donation box, you...

A. Fly across the room and yank Teddy out of her hands. There is no way you can fall asleep without him, and she knows that.

B. Take a deep breath and stash your old stuffies in the box, hoping they make it to a good home. On second thought, you pull out one fave to save on your dresser.

C. Agree and let her pack up all your plush pals—they were getting dingy anyway. It'll be good to have more space in your room.

After weeks of pleading, your little bro finally manages to get your 'rents to do family night at Chuck E. Cheese's. You...

A. Give him a high-five. Who doesn't love an evening of Skee-ball and double-cheese pizza?

B. Feel happy for the little guy and promise to show him your technique for outsmarting the claw machine.

C. Pop a few mags and some earbuds in your tote. You'll need those to get through a long—and loud—night.

Your bestie is checking out your closet floor for some shoes to wear to a school dance. First thing she finds?

A. Monkey slippers. They're so soft and cozy.

B. Booties. You love how they're trendy and functional.

C. Four-inch platform heels. They make you super tall.

You and your crew are grabbing a bite at your favorite lunch spot. You go for a...

A. Chocolate shake with extra whipped cream. Don't forget the cherry!

B. Cheeseburger with a side of sweet potato fries.

C. Quinoa salad with sliced avocado and sun-dried tomatoes.

You're chatting with your crush, thinking all is going great, when he asks if your friend Charlotte has a boyfriend. You...

A. Tell him she's into someone else. You don't know that for certain, but you need to keep him focused on you.

B. Shrug and say you're not sure who she likes these days, then excuse yourself for a bummer session.

C. Say she's a great girl and leave it at that. If that's how it's going to be, you're not about to get in the way.

The party of the year just so happens to land on the same night as your cousin's string recital, which your parents say is a mandatory event. What to do?

A. Turn on the waterworks for Dad as soon as he gets home. He has never been able to resist the power of convincing-but-insincere tears.

B. Run to your room and lock the door. You need some space, because it's gonna take you at least an hour of venting to your bestie before you get over this.

C. Ask your buds to text you all the juicy deets of the party as it unfolds, and go to the concert with your family (and you'll even try to enjoy it).

Speaking of Dad, he just told you he'll get you the tech toy of your choice as an early b-day gift. Before he changes his mind, you shoot him a link to...

A. A Nintendo DS with a Disney Princess case. You'll be able to play your favorite games, wherever you go.

B. An iPhone. You'll tell him it's so you can keep in touch with the fam. But, obviously, you'll download the occasional app or song. That's kinda the point!

C. A tablet, since you can use it for school, too. You've been meaning to switch to a digital library for, like, ever.

Your lab partner just confided in you about her first crush, and you swore up and down not to tell a soul about it. After science class, you...

A. Run to your crew and give them a full report. You can't believe she'd actually even like him!

B. Let the secret simmer for a day or two before casually mentioning it to your big sis—she won't spill it to anyone. Well, probably not.

C. Keep the scoop stowed away in your mental safe. A promise is a promise, no matter what.

MOSTLY A's: FOREVER YOUNG

Whether it's refusing to part with a Little Mermaid collection or spending your Saturday mornings with SpongeBob, you're not quite ready to grow up. And guess what—that's OK. There's nothing wrong with being a kid at heart for all of eternity. Just be careful you're not acting immature. While bratty scenes might have worked in the past, now that you're older, it's time to handle tough situations like a (young) adult.

MOSTLY B's: PERFECT TIMING

Yep, you're walking that tightrope between being a kid and being an adult, and doing an impressive job of pulling off a near-perfect balancing act. You know growing up doesn't mean you have to stop rocking your fave fuzzy slippers, but you also know when to turn your attention to your schoolwork. You're growing up gracefully, which is amazing. If you ever feel yourself veering off of the road to maturity, simply steer yourself back on track.

MOSTLY C's: BEYOND YOUR YEARS

From your taste in clothes to your refined palate, you're a sophisticated sister. It's great that you can handle all situations in such a dignified manner. But make sure you're not taking life too seriously—or missing out on some fun. Order your ice cream with sprinkles, pull on a neon tank top and challenge your sibs to a round of mini golf. You've only got a few more years left to use the "I'm a kid" excuse, so enjoy it!

WOULD YOU RATHER...?

❏ Coke **or** ❏ Sprite?

❏ Texts **or** ❏ Snaps?

❏ Christmas **or** ❏ Birthday?

❏ Movie **or** ❏ Book?

❏ Katy Perry **or** ❏ Taylor Swift?

❏ Rock **or** ❏ Hip-hop?

❏ Reading **or** ❏ Writing?

❏ Laptop **or** ❏ TV?

❏ Winter **or** ❏ Summer?

❏ Spring **or** ❏ Fall?

❏ Spending time with family **or** ❏ Spending time with friends?

❏ BF **or** ❏ Crush?

❏ BFF **or** ❏ Lotsa friends?

❏ Puppy **or** ❏ Kitten?

❏ Drawing **or** ❏ Photography?

How Technologically

Are you addicted to your phone? Or do you turn away from technology? Find out if you have the perfect balance of on-screen and off-screen time or if you need to tweak your tech routine.

When you get home from school, what's the first thing you do?

A. Head straight to the TV with a bag of chips. You need a few hours of total vegging before you can even think about doing anything else.

B. Check Instagram and catch up on your favorite blogs, of course. If that leads you down a few Internet black holes until dinner, so be it.

C. Grab a snack, then maybe spend fifteen minutes online before you get to your homework. You sneak a couple peeks at your cell but mostly stay focused.

D. No tech trances for you. Homework, a book or crafts projects are your go-to afterschool activities.

You and your friends are hangin' at your house on a Friday night. How do you spend the evening?

A. Curl up on the couch with a movie and popcorn.

B. Play video games for an hour, then begin an exhilarating round of Truth or Dare.

C. Makeovers! Then ya post the pics on Insta right away.

D. Bust out the Sorry! and play a retro fave game.

Tapped in R U?

How many hours a day do you spend watching TV?

A. Who's counting?

B. Just a couple.

C. You only watch when your fave show is on.

D. You're so busy with other stuff, you barely watch TV.

Your family is going on vacation to a tiny Carribean island. Only prob? You won't have wifi, TV or phones for a week. Do you freak out?

A. Umm, yes. How are you supposed to watch *Pretty Little Liars*? How are you supposed to communicate with your friends?

B. Kind of. Maybe you'll stop at an Internet café a couple times. And you can still watch movies, right?

C. You might feel out of the loop for a week, but it's worth it to spend quality time with your family.

D. With all the awesome sights, you won't even notice. What's a couple days unplugged?

You and your cousins are driving to see your grandparents, who live three hours away. How do you spend the drive?

A. Earbuds in, blanket over head. Maybe if you tune out everything, the drive will go by faster.

B. You host your own movie marathon. Thank goodness for the DVD player in your dad's SUV.

C. You play Candy Crush and Scrabble on your mom's iPad for a while, then chat with your little sis the rest of the way.

D. Nose in a book. Why waste precious reading time on anything else?

You're at the kitchen table eating a yummy pasta dinner with your family. Where's your phone?

A. Right next to you, of course. You like to sneakily Facebook-stalk and check your Instagram feed while you munch your meal.

B. On your lap, with the tone set to "silent." That way, you can still see if you get a text, but parents won't freak that you're not engaged in family convo.

C. In a pocket or your room. You're not exactly one to keep track of your phone at every instant of the day. The world can wait.

D. Phone? Ha, don't have one!

MOSTLY A's: DISTRACTED DIVA

You've mastered the art of playing a video game on your laptop and watching a movie on your iPad, all while Snap-chatting with your BFFs. It might be time for a serious screen-check. There's nothing wrong with technology, but don't let it distract you 24/7. Maybe go for a walk outside with your pooch, or bust out that art set you got for your birthday. Not every cool thing in this life comes with a charger, we promise.

MOSTLY B's: SCREEN QUEEN

You can handle being away from your digital life...but only when you have to. You get bored quickly when you don't have access to your phone or social media. Still, you haven't forgotten how to have old-school fun. Just watch how much time you spend in front of a screen. On your third hour of TV? Hmm, maybe find another activity. And when you're having a convo with Mom or a friend, really listen—which may mean keeping your phone stashed.

MOSTLY C's: WELL-BALANCED WATCHER

You like to KIT with friends, but you're no addict. You can stand to go without, and you understand when it's time to put the phone away and be present with your friends and family. When you do have fun in front of a screen, you like to do it with others (YouTube vids are always better with a bud, right?). But that doesn't mean you hate technology; you just get that sometimes face-to-face communication and hands-on activities are cool, too.

MOSTLY D's: TECHNO-TERRIFIED

You pretty much never bask in the light of a screen. In fact, you practically run from anything electronic. It's great that you prefer to have fun outside or with your nose buried in a book, but don't be afraid to spend some time online or chill with a movie every once in a while. There are lots of creative ways to have a great time with your friends using social media or tech. Branch out and join the rest of your crew in the 21st century!

What's Your

1. **What's your go-to after-school snack?**

A. Power bar and gallons of water. You need to refuel like crazy.

B. Trail mix. There's nothing like GORP to get you through the day.

C. Greek yogurt topped with strawberries and walnuts. So fresh.

2. **What's your ideal summer vacay?**

A. Jetting to watch a major sporting event like Wimbledon.

B. Headin' to Hawaii—surf, sand and sun!

C. Living it up at a luxurious resort, complete with a relaxing massage, mani and pedi.

3. **If you were a shoe, what would you be?**

A. Running sneakers. You're a girl who's always on the go.

B. Hiking boots. They're practical, reliable and totally waterproof.

C. Shoes? Ha! Barefoot is more my style.

4. **It's Saturday afternoon, and you're just gonna hang around the house. What are you wearing?**

A. T-shirt of your fave team and mesh shorts.

B. "Save the Earth" tee and worn-in khaki capris.

C. Hot pink tank top with your black leggings.

5. **The TV show you can't get enough of is...**

A. Anything on ESPN, duh. You can pretty much watch it for hours on end.

B. *Survivor*. The competition has nothing on your outdoorsy skills.

C. *Dancing with the Stars*. You sooo wish you could compete!

Workout Style?

MOSTLY A's: SPORTY CHICA

You've got tons of energy and you love to have fun. You're the first one on the courts and the last one to leave. Stay active even when sports are over by looking for get-pumped routines you can do at home. Cardio kickboxing, training for a triathlon or organizing a neighborhood ultimate Frisbee league are all up your alley. Lace up those sneakers and get your groove on.

MOSTLY B's: NATURE GAL

You'd live outdoors if you could. You jump at any chance to soak up some scenery, so load up your pack and get out there. Whether you're going for an early-morning trail run or biking around your 'hood, you don't need a fancy gym to get pumped. Other fitness faves to check out: indoor rock climbing, adventure races (try a mud run!) or kayaking. Slather on the SPF, then get ready to go!

MOSTLY C's: YOGA DIVA

You love feeling good about yourself, but getting all dirty and sweaty just isn't your thing. You're calm, cool and collected, so low-key stuff is your fave. Yoga and Pilates are perfect for you and definitely more on your level. To get even more in the groove, try some dance DVDs, a spin class or even karate. Don't forget to crank the cardio from time to time.

You're never satisfied with your creations in Art class, a B's alright but an A is much better, and you're fairly positive there's zero chance your crush would ever be into you. Sound familiar?

You've spent days aligning your atoms, molecules and what's-a-majigs to make the perfect molecular structure of DNA for the science fair. When the big day finally arrives, judges award you with a third-place ribbon. You...

A. Are beyond ecstatic and tie it to your backpack. Oh, everyone's gonna hear about this!

B. Call Mom to tell her the news. Your hard work paid off, and you're content with that.

C. Unravel like a double helix. All of those late nights and long hours...for third place?

Sitting in the caf, you overhear someone asking your BFF about her big b-day plans when it hits you—you totally spaced it! You...

A. Spend the rest of the day writing up cute IOU coupons to gift her. Hey, her birthday's not over yet.

B. Pull your bestie aside and confess you forgot. You'll take her out tonight to make it up to her.

C. Feel so, so, SO bad. You're totally the worst friend ever on earth. You barely finish your sandwich before bursting into tears over your mistake.

Dolled up and glammed out for the Spring Fling, you do one final mirror check before heading out the door. What do you see?

A. You, smiling. Your skin looks amazing. You love your dress. Your hair happens to be perfecto.

B. Maybe a tad too much blush, but overall, not too bad if you may say so yourself.

C. Your eyeliner already smudging, armpit poodge and hair suffering from an attack of the frizzies.

Your soccer team made it to the finals of a huge state tourney. As the clock ticks down, you take a shot to score the game-tying goal and...miss. Your reaction?

A. Shrug your shoulders and commiserate with your teammates. Tough loss, but you played your best.

B. Put your head down and sprint to the sidelines to grab some water while fighting back a few tears. Then make a promise to yourself to hit the field after school tomorrow for extra shooting time.

C. Crumple to the ground and bury your head in your hands. You had a shot and blew it, big time.

You just auditioned for the spring musical and are really hoping to land a part. When Mom asks you how it went, you...

A. Tell her it's in the bag and ask to stop at Starbucks on the way home. To frapp or not to frapp, that is the more pressing question.

B. Say you're just not sure. Parts of it went well, but then that dance number they taught you was tricky.

C. Cringe while replaying the audition in your head. You should've read the lines this way, not that way.

You just got back from a vacay with your family to find out your bestie's grandpa died. She was absolutely devastated, and you weren't there for her. You...

A. Tell her you're so sorry and plan a sleepover to chat. You always know how to cheer her right up.

B. Give her a big hug and ask if she wants to talk about it. Thankfully, you're there now.

C. Can't believe you had fun while your soul sister was cooped up in her room crying. You owe her.

You and your girls snag invites to a party Friday night. You're having a blast playing games and mingling with the crowd when you spot one of your friends sitting in the corner solo and sulking. You...

A. Roll your eyes. She's always ruining your good time, and you wish she'd lighten up.

B. Run over and asks if she wants to join your convo. You've extended the invite, so it's up to her now.

C. Spend the rest of the night in the corner with her. If she's not having fun, you can't either.

The cutest guy in school suddenly plops his lunch tray next to you in the caf and asks if he can sit there. Your reaction is...

A. You feel like you've just won the crush lottery. You can't believe he's into you. Well, actually, yes you can.

B. Stop yourself from getting your hopes up. You're not gonna jump to conclusions—he could just want to copy your homework.

C. Look around for the hidden cameras. Is this some sort of prank or something? You're not amused.

MOSTLY A's: EASY BREEZY

You look in the mirror and like what you see. You hardly ever stress and know there's no use dwelling on mistakes when you make 'em. Props to you for having major confidence! Just make sure you keep yourself challenged and don't let yourself off the hook too easily if you really screw up. Then, take your attitude and spread the good vibes, girl! If you notice a bud being too hard on herself, let her in on your stress-less secrets. So inspiring!

MOSTLY B's: JUST TOUGH ENOUGH

When it comes to goof-ups, you're not too hard on yourself. You might feel horrible if you slight a friend, but hey, everybody trips up on occasion, right? And maybe you didn't get that A you were seeking, but a B+ isn't so bad. By having a solid understanding that everyone flubs once in a while and it's normal to have a bad day, you're able to keep a smile on your face. Keep that approach, and you'll be able to handle any challenge that comes your way.

MOSTLY C's: FAR TOO HARD

Ever stop and think you're waaay too tough on yourself? We do! Whether you're beating yourself up over a slightly imperfect performance or doubting your abilities as a friend, it's time to show yourself some love. Start by setting your standards slightly lower. You might need to take a step back to realize you don't always have to be flawless. God loves you exactly the way you are. And nothing you do can ever make him love you more. Or less.

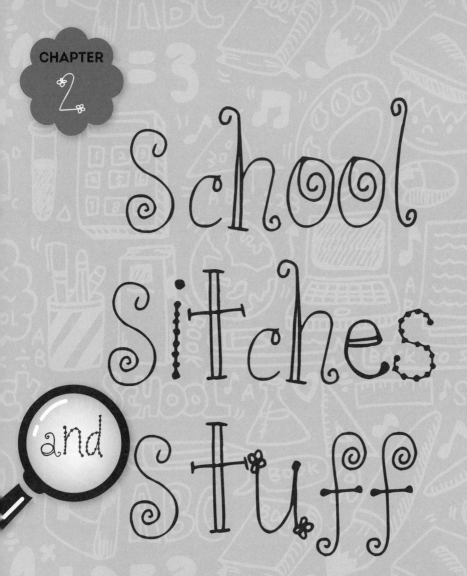

School Sitches and Stuff

Navigating the ins and outs of school can feel overwhelming, but classes and extracurrics don't have to leave you a stress mess. Learn to study more efficiently and feel less frazzled, once and for all!

What's Your

Class is in session, so where are you? Hanging on your teacher's every word, or hanging in the back passing notes? Take this quiz to uncover your secret studying style, then read on for tips that'll zip you to the head of the class—stat.

Phew! You just started middle school. You can tell us: How's it going so far?

A. Great! You've looked forward to this for a long time, so you're set.

B. Pretty good. Algebra might be rough, but your music class is totally fun.

C. Ugh. Could the school day be any longer? And you have, like, six hours of homework every night.

Time to present a big group project. Right before you're set to go, one of your group members, Matt, tells you he forgot his notecards on his kitchen table. Eeps! What are you going to do now, girl?

A. Take over for him. You reviewed all of the talking points just in case, so you're comfy handling his part—and everyone else's if you have to.

B. Request to reschedule for tomorrow. If that doesn't fly, you and the rest of the group will have to pitch in with Matt's section.

C. Let him wing it. He can probably make up something last minute, right?!

School Stance!

Why is art your fave class?

A. It's an easy A. Gotta keep that GPA up.

B. You love to paint, duh! You'd take art all day if you had your way.

C. You sit right next to your BFF, so you can chat while you craft. Plus, you've got a prime view of the cute new guy.

You're taking a monstrous math exam when you notice Mia, the girl next you, sneaking glances at your laptop screen. How do you handle it?

A. Raise your hand and call the teacher over ASAP. No one's going to steal your answers.

B. Switch your laptop to the other side of your desk and shoot her a look. If she keeps it up, you'll clue your teacher in on her cheating ways.

C. You move your screen out of her sight and forget about it. You almost understand why she'd copy—the test is totally impossible.

You've got sixth-period study hall. How do you spend the time?

A. Studying, of course. And if you're done with everything? You'll read ahead or do extra-credit work.

B. Depends on the day. If you're swamped, you'll get a head start on your HW. But if your plate's empty, you grab a mag and chill out.

C. You listen to music, snooze or get a cookie from the caf. Homework can wait.

Uh-oh, you're not doing so hot on Mrs. Miller's pop history quizzes. How do you handle?

A. March right up to Miller and ask her how you can remedy this situation. There's no way you're going to let C's and D's ruin your class rank.

B. Start a study sheet with notes on stuff that might show up. If there's a chapter you didn't get, you'll raise your hand...a lot.

C. You blow off the bad marks. Pop quizzes don't count that much toward your overall grade, right?

You've got a major science project due on Monday. It's Saturday—what's the status?

A. Almost done. You're just waiting for the paint to dry on your visual aids, and then you'll do a few practice runs to make sure everything's just right.

B. Getting there. The research is finished, and you've bought the materials. Now, you just have to put it all together—but that can wait 'til tomorrow.

C. Psssh, Saturday is *so* the day to do nothing. Sure, you have a few ideas, but you've still got a whole 48 hours to get it all done!

Your friend Amber just asked you to go to a movie with her on Tuesday night. The only prob? That English exam on Wednesday. What do you tell her?

A. You'd love to go...on another night. As fun as that sounds, studying comes first.

B. The movie's not 'til 7. You can study 'til 6, go out, then read things over one last time before bed.

C. Yes, obviously. You've been dying to see that new flick, and you can do a quick cram tomorrow.

MOSTLY A's:
Super Studious Sweetie

You're a serious student—and have the glowing GPA to prove it. But make sure you're not sacrificing your sanity as you gun for those grades. Try scheduling some breaks into your workload, like a mid-week dinner with your girls or an evening jog with your pooch. And remember that once in a while, it's OK to go out and do something special. Keeping things lighter will prevent you from crashing and burning before the semester is over.

MOSTLY B's:
Balanced Babe

Um, did somebody say "well-rounded student"? That's totally you. You know that grades are key, but you've also factored in time for other activities, your friends and yourself. You've got a good thing going, but don't be afraid to step up your studying style just a tad. Challenge yourself by exiting your comfort zone. Scared of public speaking? Overcome that fear by offering to be the moderator for your next group project. Keep up the good work!

MOSTLY C's:
Slackin' Sistah

Settling for so-so in school? So not OK. Time for an attitude adjustment. You've only got one shot at school (unless you're into repeating grades), so make it count. Buckle down and study up. Don't be afraid to ask for extra help from your teachers—do that now before you're in too deep. Then, dedicate a block of time for hitting the books each night (no texts, no exceptions!). You'll still be able to squeeze in fun after you're done studying, promise.

7 WAYS TO SUCCEED IN SCHOOL

1. MAKE GETTING GREAT GRADES MORE FUN
One idea? Throw a study party. Invite pals over for a fiesta before the big Spanish test, talking only *en Español*.

2. MIX IT UP
Switch up your study style to keep from getting stuck in a rut. Try making your own multiple-choice practice tests to see what you retained. Studying in a group? Bounce ideas around by quizzing each other, game show-style.

3. GET OH-SO ORGANIZED
Get a handle on heaps of homework by tracking assignments in a planner or Google calendar. Then, de-clutter your desk (a messy workspace distracts) and surround yourself with motivating mementos, like a test you rocked or inspirational quotes to give your mood an insta-boost.

4. TUNE IN
Surprisingly, music makes a great study buddy. Just keep the volume down and stick to soothing, low-key stuff.

5. STEER CLEAR OF CRAMMING
Space out your workload by chipping away at big assignments as soon as you get 'em (try writing a couple of paragraphs or studying a section per night). Then, leave the night-of for a final review—and relaxing!

6. ASK FOR HELP
It's not always easy to get your most pressing Qs in during class time, so try stopping by after school for a one-on-one with your teacher so she can pinpoint where you're tripping up.

7. REWARD YOURSELF
Gotta read a snore-worthy history chapter? Plan to dig into your fave dish or gab on the phone with a pal when you finish up. Knowing what awaits you could be just the motivation you need to put that paper to rest.

Can You Take the Pressure?

Your parents expect straight A's. Your coach says you're not "playing up to your potential." Your teachers tell you it's time to "apply yourself better." Your friends say, "It's no big deal. Just do it!" Life is full of pressure. Question is, how well do you deal with it? Test your coping skills, then check out our tips on nixing crazy stress.

You're totally zoned out in history class, contemplating whether you'll go for pizza or mac-n-cheese at lunch, when the teacher calls your name. Everyone is staring. You...

A. Blurt, "1862! Abraham Lincoln! The Spanish Armada!"

B. Ask the teacher to please repeat the question.

C. Ask a question about the Civil Rights Movement. Even if Teach was talking about something totally different, Martin Luther King, Jr. is her favorite topic and a surefire diversion tactic.

D. Look back blankly and say, "I don't have a clue."

It's time for your poetry reading. You've practiced your lines so many times you could say them backward...in pig Latin...while juggling kiwis. What do you do when your teacher asks for a volunteer to go first?

A. Duck behind the girl sitting in front of you.

B. Charge the podium.

C. Choose that moment to visit the bathroom—you need a breather already.

D. Run out of class. You'll apologize later.

You're at your school's biggest bash of the year, and word around the gym is that your crush wants you to ask him to dance. You...

A. Wonder where the nearest trash can is—you feel sick all of a sudden.

B. Weave your way through the crowd to find your crush. You figure the worst he can do is say "no."

C. Tell your friends you'll consider it. Maybe if you wait long enough, they'll all forget about it before the night ends.

D. Think to yourself, "No way." If he wants to dance, he can ask you himself.

It's the last game of the season for your basketball rec team, and you're down by one basket. There are only 10 seconds left on the clock, and your teammate just passed you the ball. You...

A. Immediately pass the ball off to another teammate. You don't want that kind of pressure.

B. Turn to the basket and take a shot. It's your team's only chance to win the game!

C. Dribble the ball as close to the basket as you can get, stalling to avoid that terrible moment when you shoot, miss and humiliate yourself.

D. Drop the ball like it's hot. It rolls out of bounds just as the buzzer goes off, but at least the pressure is over now.

You tried your hardest in math class all semester—and scored a C-minus on your report card. You know your parents will be disappointed, especially since your older sister breezes through math with straight A's every year. On report card day, you...

A. Gnaw your nails and try to think of a way to convince your teacher to bump up your grade. Maybe you can wash her car?

B. Sign up for an after-school math tutor—that'll show your parents you seriously want to improve.

C. "Accidentally" miss the bus and walk the three miles home—you're in no hurry.

D. Tell your buds to count you out for the next 100 weekends—your social life is o-o-o-ver.

MOSTLY A's: Stressed Señorita

Do yourself a favor and don't try to be Supergirl. You're probably very talented, with lots of interests, and that's great. But no one can do it all—and no one can do it perfectly. Before taking on new responsibilities, think things through logically: Do you have enough time and energy to handle it? Learn to say no to some things—even activities you enjoy—and be realistic about your expectations and goals. Take some time to think about who you are and what you believe, so you'll be ready when your ideas are challenged and things don't go your way. Preparation will help you stay calm when crunch time rolls around.

MOSTLY B's: **Confident Chick**

You don't just handle pressure—you thrive on it. You're always up for a challenge. In fact, the higher the stakes, the better. But a word of caution: People like you sometimes procrastinate since they like that last-minute adrenaline rush. It's great you can work well under pressure, but putting everything off 'til the last minute will land you in trouble if you're not careful. It's great to have self-confidence, but watch out if you start thinking you're superior to everyone else. You can always learn something from others.

MOSTLY C's: **Procrastination Princess**

You see pressure coming—and head the other way. Maybe you avoid conflict because you're afraid of offending people, but the truth is you can't dodge everything in life. Some big decisions require serious think time, but there will be other occasions when you might not have much time to contemplate about your choice. Do the best you can with the information you have. You'll rarely be 100% certain about anything, so get used to it. Be decisive anyway.

MOSTLY D's: **Give-Up Girl**

Yeah, sure, trying new things can be scary, we get it. But how'll you know what you're good at if you don't give it a shot? As you discover your strengths, you'll enjoy the excitement that goes along with success. Bombed at piano? Fine, it's not your gig—move on to something else. You can avoid pressure by not allowing others to talk you into stuff you don't want to do. Practice standing strong on the little things—like defending the kid on the bus who always gets teased—so you'll be prepared when bigger tests in life come along.

6 GREAT WAYS
to stay cool in the pressure cooker

1. Repeat Philippians 4:13: "I can do all this through him who gives me strength." Say it 'til you believe it!

2. Take care of your body. Exercise, eat healthy and get plenty of sleep. You'll handle stress better if your body's in good condition.

3. Squash the perfectionist monster. No one does anything perfectly. No one. Why expect the impossible?

4. Learn to say no. Simple, straightforward and sometimes totally necessary if you're feeling pressured to do something that isn't right for you. If a firm no doesn't do the trick, try changing the subject or making a quick exit.

5. **Journal. Writing your feelings will help you sort out your emotions and relieve stress.**

6. Talk about it. If possible, find someone who's been through a similar situation and ask how she handled it. Even if she can't offer some super simple solution, it always helps to have support.

What's Your Secret

Your locker's crammed with books and your planner's packed with assignments. So what's the best way to stuff your noggin with knowledge without going into overload? Take this quiz to find out your own learning style and sail through the semester.

You promised to whip up a batch of brownies for next week's Student Gov sweets sale. You're a great cook, but you don't know the first thing about baking. You...

A. Hit up YouTube and watch a detailed how-to video on double-fudge bars.

B. Scour the kitchen for Mom's Barefoot Contessa cookbook, then read each step aloud before you even crack an egg.

C. Grab Grandma—and her blue-ribbon recipe. Have her set out and measure the ingredients while you fish out the baking pan.

D. Throw on an apron and dig right in. So what if the first two batches are a bust? Third time's a charm.

Your fam is heading to Paris for spring break. How do you prep for the trip?

A. Create a PowerPoint slideshow with pretty pics—and pronunciations—of popular Parisian sights, like La Tour d'Eiffel and Versailles.

B. Download a few different French-language podcasts and listen to them each night before bed.

Learning Style?

C. Enlist your BFF as your French study buddy. Have her over once a week to practice parlez-ing Français while indulging in homemade crêpes. Ooh la la!

D. Take a DIY approach, from renting a French flick (no subtitles for you!) to checking out French newspapers and fashion mags in the library.

Dad's driving you to a new bud's house for a sleepover. How do you direct him to her place?

A. By landmarks: past the new shopping center, left at the school, then turn onto the first street past the post office.

B. Call her up and have her tell you how to get there while repeating it to Pops.

C. Find her street on Google Maps and navigate with point-to-point directions.

D. Just wing it. You're pretty sure she lives on the other side of Baker Street, but if you see a sign that says "Welcome to Canada," you'll know to turn around.

Your class takes a field trip to the aquarium. As soon as the group walks through the doors, you...

A. Hit up the amphibian room to read the bulleted facts and figures alongside each tank.

B. Listen closely as the tour guide tells you about each exotic fish and their natural habitat.

C. Make a beeline to scope out the hands-on tank. You can't wait to pet a stingray.

D. Ignore the tour and roam around. You'd much rather see penguins than piranhas, anyway.

The freshman mixer is almost here. When it comes time to hit the dance floor, what will you do?

A. Watch what everyone else is doing before you join in.

B. Wait until the Cha Cha Slide starts playing. You'll slide to the left when the music says so.

C. Wow everyone with your moves while encouraging your friends to get out there with you.

D. Dance like no one's watching. Two left feet? So not a prob for you.

You're giving an oral report on the Irish potato famine in history class next week. To make sure you've got it down, you...

A. Rewrite your speech over and over again to help you memorize it.

B. Record yourself reciting it, then play it back a bunch of times 'til you're completely down with all the key facts and dates.

C. Do a "dress rehearsal." Ask your parents to be the "audience" as you walk through every step, from index cards to eye contact.

D. Review your notes the night before, then just go for it. If you draw a blank, you'll just encourage a little class participation!

You're at the mall and just spotted an old friend from elementary school. The first thing that jumps to your mind about her is...

A. That adorable dress she wore to the sixth-grade farewell dance.

B. Her high-pitched voice and contagious laugh.

C. The moves to the dance you two choreographed for a second-grade talent show.

D. Um, not much. Her name is Lisa, right? Or is it Lindsey? Something that starts with "L"...

Like it or not, it's time to dissect a frog for anatomy, and you need an A on this or your parents will flip. With your lab partner by your side, what's your best plan of action?

A. Watch your teacher's every move during the demo while taking meticulous notes.

B. Meet up with your partner after class to talk through each step of the dissection.

C. Practice by dissecting everything in sight, from your grapefruit right down to your Twix bar.

D. Quickly go over the steps before class then, well... sorry, Kermit.

MOSTLY A's: The Eyes Have It

You absorb everything visually, meaning you can't quite grasp a concept unless you actually see it. So instead of listening to your teacher explain how to fire up that Bunsen burner, you'd prefer to watch her do it, then try for yourself.

SUCCESS STRATEGY: You need an unobstructed view of your teacher's every move, so snag a seat at the front of class. Then jot notes while listening to lectures, and draw diagrams or charts to help you understand key concepts.

BEST TEST TRICK: Make a checklist of everything you've gotta cover for the next exam—seeing it out on paper will help you focus. Also, highlight your notes in different colors (to group together key points) or rewrite them (repeatedly seeing the words embeds them in your memory). If you blank on a question at test time? Close your eyes and visualize where that info was on your outline—it'll come back to you.

MOSTLY B's: All Ears

You learn through listening. Always alert, you quickly pick up new concepts by hearing someone speak or by reading them aloud. No wonder you memorize the words to every new hit song the first time you hear it!

SUCCESS STRATEGY: No distractions—you need to listen up to grasp everything the teacher is telling you. If you can't hear the lectures, inch closer to the front of the room, and don't be afraid to ask her to repeat anything you might have missed. The more you hear, the better you'll do. Trust us!

BEST TEST TRICK: Rally a study group for review. Talk out the concepts with each other and come up with short songs for each theory or equation so you can sing 'em to yourself come test time. And as you're reviewing your notes, read them aloud to yourself to be sure all of the info sticks.

MOSTLY C's: **All About Action**

You learn through experience. You're the first to shout, "Let me try!" and are always willing to jump right in.

SUCCESS STRATEGY: You're an action-seeker who does best in classes that involve physical tasks (think gym or drama). But when it comes to strictly exercising your brain, class time can be a bit of a bore for you. So spark up the sedentary stuff by volunteering to read chapters out loud or to lead the chemistry class demo.

BEST TEST TRICK: Act out events you're reading about (grab two tennis balls to reenact smashing atoms), or walk around while memorizing stats. And give your brain breaks by studying in short chunks of time. Try 15 to 20 minute blocks, with a three-minute break in between. Alternating between activity and rest will really help your concentration.

MOSTLY D's: **Self-Taught Student**

You learn through experimentation. A curious chica, you love to test yourself with tons of trial and error, gleaning valuable lessons from mistakes as you go along.

SUCCESS STRATEGY: Just because you shine in the art of self-teaching doesn't mean you can snooze through the semester. Challenge yourself by setting up a list of goals to go after, like finally snagging that A in English. Then come up with your own ways to make sure you see them through, and offer yourself a sweet reward when you do.

BEST TEST TRICK: Since you work best on your own, opt to study independently. Take practice quizzes, or flip through stacks of flashcards at night. And if you can't quite wrap your head around a concept, call up a classmate to discuss—don't let your independence get in the way of asking for help when you need it.

Has Gossip Got

Some nuggets of gold are just too good to keep to yourself, right? When it comes to juicy info, can you keep your lips zipped, or are you too quick to dish the deets to anyone who will listen? This quiz will reveal if the world's secrets are safe with you.

You're stuck playing monkey in the middle during a friendship feud. When each bestie calls you up for a vent session, you...

A. Call foul on both parties by spilling the details on who said what. With everything out in the open, you're sure they'll forgive 'n' forget.

B. Pretend like you're on the side of whomever is talking but don't disclose any super mean words.

C. Listen to each grumble, then tell your friends that they're really better off talking to each other about their issues, not you.

Have you ever had your reputation put through the school's rumor mill?

A. Yes, and you didn't mind. That meant your name was on everybody's lips!

B. Once, but nothing serious, thank goodness. Being at the center of snickers and stares = total nightmare.

C. Nope, and you'd be surprised if it were to happen... ever. You tend to stay far away from silly drama.

You Gripped?

You roll outta bed on Saturday, and the first thing you check is...

A. Your favorite entertainment news website. Gotta have a daily dose of Hollywood happenings.

B. Instagram. It's your #1 go-to for what's up with your friends and fam. Plus, you like to see what the fashionistas at your school are getting into.

C. Texts. You're expecting to hear from your BFF about afternoon plans.

Your partner in gym class confesses her crush on the new cutie. You...

A. Ask one of his friends if the feelings are mutual. Sure, she swore you to secrecy, but you're trying to help her out.

B. Keep your lips zipped...except to five of your closest friends, of course.

C. Vow to never tell a soul then actually, ahem, *never tell a soul*.

The minute you get home from the biggest birthday party of the year, your little sister bombards you with 20 questions—she wants to hear *all* about it. You...

A. Give her a moment-by-moment recap, including the look on the birthday girl's face when she slipped on some spilled punch. Who's Sis gonna tell?

B. Go into detail about what everyone was wearing. You know how much she loves a red carpet moment.

C. Tell her the basics of the evening, then turn the tables and ask about her night.

When it comes to celeb gossip...

A. You "Like" and "Follow" from your phone. You've gotta know it all, the second it happens.

B. You usually get the details from your bestie about breakups and makeups of celeb duos.

C. You just don't care. You have volleyball tryouts in two weeks—that's all that matters right now.

Rumor has it the class clown Ryan confessed his love for quiet little Annabelle last week. How do you get the details?

A. Ask around. Somebody is sure to have some info.

B. Try to decipher their body language the next time you spot them chatting in the halls.

C. You don't. It's none of your business.

Waiting for your ride after school, you overhear some older kids dishing dirt about your big sister. You...

A. Wait a day then start spilling about them in retaliation. That'll show 'em.

B. Bust your way into their conversation and tell them what you really think of them. Which isn't much.

C. Politely tell the bullies you don't appreciate them talking about your sister like that. Then drop it.

Your neighbor confesses he has a teeny crush on your friend and asks you not to say a word. You...

A. Slyly pull out your cell and shoot her a text before he's even done talking.

B. Casually bring him up the next time you're chilling with your friend and flash her a knowing smile. You haven't said anything, technically, but she'll probably figure it out.

C. Keep mum until he asks you for help. Then maybe you'll drop a hint or two.

Your cheer captain got booted from the team after she flunked Spanish, but she's telling everyone she punted her pompoms because she just didn't feel like being part of the squad anymore. You...

A. Call her out and tell everyone the scoop. You need to protect your team's rep. You girls work beyond hard and getting good grades is just part of it.

B. Roll your eyes and privately tell a couple of your buds the real deal. You two are kinda-sorta friends, so it's not worth making her feel even more miserable.

C. Just let it go. You know she's totally embarrassed, and you don't want her to feel worse.

MOSTLY A's: Gossip Addict

Hey, gossip girl. From who's dating whom to all of the weekend parties, you're always in the know. Your girls come to you when they want some scoop, but may find it hard to shell out their deepest and darkest. Spilling secrets and talking behind backs almost always leads to hurt feelings. Keep your loose lips in check by putting yourself in others' shoes. The next time you feel the itch to dish, change the subject or find something kind to say instead.

MOSTLY B's: Rationalizing Reteller

You're not shouting people's secrets all over town—but you're not exactly keeping mum, either. Careful: it's a fine line you're walking, and you're bound to fall over the edge eventually. Just because you're not as gossipy as some doesn't mean you're good to go. A well-timed kind word instead of a not-so-nice factoid might just make someone's day.

MOSTLY C's: Silence is Golden

You're the go-to girl for secrets because your buds know you'll keep them, no matter what. Kudos for being so trustworthy. Girls like you understand what King Solomon wrote in Proverbs 21:23: "Those who guard their mouths and their tongues keep themselves from [trouble]." Of course, there are some times when it's better to speak up than stay silent—like when your sister is being targeted.

3 TIPS FOR SEALED LIPS

1. **WAIT ON IT.** Take a couple minutes, hours or even days to let it sit. Chances are, after the initial desire to blab goes away, you'll be able to keep the secret.

2. **PRAY ABOUT IT.** A gossip betrays a confidence, but a trustworthy person keeps a secret. (Proverbs 11:13)

3. **THINK ABOUT IT.** Is it ever OK to tell, even if you promised to keep a friend's secret? If something is seriously wrong or someone is being hurt, then it might be smart to tell a parent or trusted adult.

What's Your Competition Position?

Ah, victory—you got your first taste of it when you were five and whomped your sister in a legendary Candyland grudge match. Ever since then, you'll do whatever it takes to win big. Which is all good—right? Well, it all depends. Take this quiz to figure out if you've got the right kind of fight.

Your soccer team is fighting tooth and nail in a tough tie breaker against your school's biggest rival. Finally, it looks like your side is gonna pull it out—until Emily, your goalie, misses a block and the other team wins. What do you say to Emily as you both walk off the field?

A. "Were you tired or something? That looked like an easy block, and we really needed this win."

B. "Don't feel bad, Em. It was rough out there for everybody. They were a tough team, and you did your best."

C. "I'd never want to be goalie—it's just way too much responsibility. I don't really know why you or anyone else would wanna do it."

Your friend Gracie is telling everyone about the new ice cream place, and she keeps calling it the Cream Team. You're sure it's called the Cream Dream, but when you tell her, she refuses to believe you. What do you do?

A. Shrug it off. It's not that important.

B. Immediately look it up on the Internet, so you can prove to Gracie that she's wrong, and you're right.

C. Ask your friends what they think and then give Gracie a smug look when they take your side.

Everybody knows your sister Ashley is an amazing singer—she even performs at weddings in your home-town. So what talent are you trying to develop?

A. Good question. You've been a little intimidated by Super Sis, but hey, it's time to finally figure out your shining talent.

B. Drawing. You think the sketches you do are actually pretty cool.

C. Singing, too, of course. Anything Ashley can do, you can do better.

You and your friend Dylan are heavy into a Monopoly bout when you land on Park Place. You are so winning this thing! So what's your next move?

A. Shriek with delight, claim your victory and make sure to tell all his friends about it at school the next day.

B. You cut to the chase, wrap up the win and say, "Now who's the reigning champ, mister?"

C. You go for the win, then smile. "Good game. That was a close one."

It's down to you and Ava for the lead in your school's production of *Annie*. You dash to the bulletin board as the cast list goes up—and find out she'll be wearing the orange curls. What's your first thought?

A. "I can't believe it! I know I was the best—it's gotta be because Ava's president of the drama club."

B. "That's a total bummer. But I've gotta be honest with myself—Ava's singing *was* stronger than mine."

C. "Guess I've got to work on my acting before the spring musical tryouts. I'll be better than Ava by then."

Your brain is screaming from attempting to learn every single word that could possibly be used in the school spelling bee. Then, you happen to spot a copy of the oh-so-secret word list in your English teacher's recycling bin. 'Fess up: Would you fish out the list if you won't get caught?

A. Not in a zillion years. You're following the rules, fair and square.

B. Maybe just this once...

C. Nah—just looking at your friends after you beat them by cheating would make you totally queasy with guilt.

At your family's annual reunion, your uncle organizes a 100-yard dash and pits you against your 6-year-old cousin, Jared. So what's your race plan?

A. You're gonna let Jared win, of course. He's the baby of the family and there's no use in whomping him.

B. You're gonna beat Jared, big-time. You'd never give up a win, even to a kid.

C. You'll see what happens—Jared might be faster than you think. You'll let him get close, but maybe you'll beat him by half a second at the end.

Amelia is the most perfect girl in your whole grade. She has a gorgeous wardrobe and awesome hair, plus she's on the dance team with a straight-A average. Today in the caf, she slipped on some sloppy joe sauce and took the most embarrassing fall. What was your reaction?

A. You looked the other way. You find it really awkward to see a total rockstar like Amelia do anything less than amazing.

B. You smiled to yourself, but didn't say anything to anyone. You don't wanna be mean, but hey, this proves she's human after all.

C. You dashed over to help her up and gave her your sweatshirt to tie around her waist to cover the sloppy joe sauce all over the back of her super cute skirt.

Your BFF dragged her dad's old air hockey table from the garage and just challenged you and your friends to a mega tournament. How do you feel going into the first round?

A. You've never played on a relic like this before, so you're bound to stink, but who cares?

B. You're sort of nervous about your skill level, but who knows? Maybe the other girls will be even worse.

C. You refuse to go first. You're not going to play until you watch a few rounds and learn from the other girls' mistakes. Hey, you're gonna do your research.

You talked your friends into trying out that crazy tough new spin class at the gym. Oddly enough, your girl Ella is a total pro, while you're barely able to catch your breath. When the teacher starts cheering Ella on for being such an amazing first-timer, you...

A. Let out a big whoopie! You're stoked someone is able to keep up, because it certainly isn't you.

B. Unclip your shoes and hightail it to the door. You give Ella a thumbs up and then mouth "headache" while pointing to your noggin. You'll meet her in the locker room, after she's had her moment in the spotlight.

C. High-five your girl and then start peddling faster. If you just try a little harder...

When it comes to life, are you happy to be in the game, or is winning the only option?

1.	A. 3	B. 2	C. 1
2.	A. 1	B. 3	C. 2
3.	A. 1	B. 2	C. 3
4.	A. 3	B. 2	C. 1
5.	A. 3	B. 1	C. 2
6.	A. 2	B. 3	C. 1
7.	A. 1	B. 3	C. 2
8.	A. 1	B. 2	C. 3
9.	A. 1	B. 3	C. 2
10.	A. 1	B. 3	C. 2

10-17 POINTS
WINNING ISN'T ALL THAT

You're all about having a good time when you're competing, and you want to make sure everyone else is having a good time, too—even if they're on the other team. You're sensitive to the feelings of others and prize loyalty and kindness more than a fleeting victory. Keep up the good work! You get that sometimes being a winner is about doing the right thing—not standing at the top of the podium. And that makes you a true champion!

25-30 POINTS
VICTORY IS SOMEWHAT SWEET

You like to win, no doubt about it, but you're not going to have a melt-down if you don't. Yep, winning isn't everything, but be careful. Even if you're not as crushed about a loss as the next girl, it's still possible you're not being as gracious as you could. Make sure the words you speak to the competition are kind, and steer clear of bragging. People will notice when you have a bad attitude, even if you're trying to keep it under wraps.

25-30 POINTS
CONQUER AT ALL COSTS

You *love* to come out on top. You're a fierce competitor, but have you ever stopped and thought what you might be losing by winning all the time? Instead of focusing so hard on the end game, shift your point of view to the fun of working to-ward what you want—like getting to spend time with your friends or improving your tennis serve. At the end of the day, it's a whole lot better to make God proud with your selfless actions than to snag a trophy.

THINK QUICK!

For this quiz, write the first word that comes to mind when you see the question-word. For example, question 1 says "blue." If the first word you think of is "sky," then write that down.

1. Blue _____

2. Hearts _____

3. American Flag_____

4. Turkey_____

5. Bugs_____

6. Paris_____

7. Ashley_____

8. Lip Gloss_____

9. Perfect_____

10. Calculator_____

11. The Number 3_____

12. Notebook_____

13. Fruit_____

14. Pick-up Lines_____

15. Quizzes _____

Are you absolutely brilliant with bucks? Or are ya still, um, trying to make cents of money? Figure out if you're too frivolous with your dough, or if you need to loosen up those purse strings.

You've been stashing your savings for weeks when some amazing strappy sandals catch your eye. Buying them will practically zero out your bank account, but they're sooo cute. You...

A. Plunk down most of your pennies on the shoes. How can you resist?

B. Admire them from afar, but keep on walking. You've worked too hard to dip into those dollars.

C. Try them on just for fun then promise yourself you'll pick them up as soon as they go on sale.

You're out to eat with your friends. Since your wallet's a little light, you're just going to order an appetizer. So what do you do when your buds decide to go all out with dinner and dessert?

A. Give in and go for a pricey pasta and chocolate cheesecake. You only live once, right?

B. Tell them you promised to have dinner at home later with your parents and stick to your original plan to kick in $5 for your share of the mozzarella sticks.

C. Order an entrée but skip dessert, saying you just couldn't squeeze more in there.

ash-itude?

3

You're just dying to go to sleepaway soccer camp this summer, but your parents are balking at the hefty price tag. What's your opinion on chipping in at least a portion of the cost?

A. You contribute whatever you can scrape together and ask your parents for the rest. You're pretty positive they'll come through.

B. You babysit for your neighbors every chance you get, including every weekend. So what if you never see your friends again? At least you'll have mad soccer skills by summer's end!

C. You cut out all the little extras, like movie popcorn and coffeehouse cappuccinos, and start saving ASAP. You figure it'll take a while for the bucks to add up, so there's no point in stalling.

4

Ka-ching! You won the raffle at the student council's annual fund-raiser. What do you do with the loot?

A. Buy candy apples and friendship bracelets for all your buds, a cute scarf for yourself and one for Mom. Hey, you didn't expect the bonus, so there's no harm in blowing it.

B. Treat your best friend to your once-a-year tradition of chili dogs and fries at the Shake Shack, and then close that wallet for good.

C. Put the cash in your purse, then call your dad for a ride. You wouldn't really be tempted to spend it, but why risk it?

It's spring, sweetie. Do you still have any of the money you raked in over Christmas?

A. Yeah, right! You'd blown those bucks by New Year's Eve. A sparkly dress and a new purse were all yours.

B. Of course. It's been socked away for something really special. Who knows? Maybe you won't even spend it until it's time for your first car or college.

C. About half—you sprang for the sweater you really wanted, and then squirreled away the rest in your savings account.

MOSTLY A's:
SPENDING QUEEN

You're a fun-loving girl who lives to be in the moment, which makes you a blast to hang with. When it comes to cash, though, you tend to blow your bucks on frivolous stuff, like lattes and trendy clothes. To stall your spendy ways, try hanging on to your money until you find something you really want. Saving for a big item may take time and patience, but it's so satisfying when you've finally reached that goal.

MOSTLY B's:
PRACTICAL PRINCESS

Wise with your wallet, you're super cautious about managing your money. This is a great skill to develop, especially while you're young. Don't be afraid to spend a li'l bit here and there, though. Budget for a fun splurge every couple of weeks—a new playlist on iTunes, cute hoop earrings or lunch out with your friends. That way you can still let loose a bit without breaking the bank.

MOSTLY C's:
DUCHESS OF DOLLARS

You go with your gut and trust your instincts, giving you a balanced perspective on what's worthy enough to cost you your well-deserved dollars. You aren't afraid to part with your pennies if the price is right, but you thoroughly think through big-ticket purchases. Whether you splurge or not, you keep the true value of money in perspective.

Besties, and Boys other Bafflers

You and your bestie are so close you know everything about each other, right? Flip the page and find out more about you and your crew, like which cutie deserves an upgrade from crush status.

You and your bestie are super tight: You know all the details about the cutie she's crushing on and the exact fro-yo flavor combo she craves. But beyond that, are you truly in the know about your BFF?

Here's how to find out:

Take this quiz together with each of ya answering for one another. When you're done, compare quizzes and tally up how many you guessed right. You may nail 'em all, or realize you're missing some essential info—either way, you'll learn plenty about your pal!

All About Your Bestie
(Circle the answer she'd pick)

Beach **OR** Mountain?

Concert **OR** Movie?

Cotton candy **OR** Funnel cake?

Glitter nail polish **OR** Fruity lip gloss?

Strawberry smoothie **OR** Chocolate milkshake?

Sleepover **OR** Sleepaway camp?

Softball **OR** Soccer?

DIY **OR** Buy?

Truth **OR** Dare?

Instagram **OR** Snapchat?

Roller skates **OR** Ice skates?

Glitzy glam **OR** Cute and pretty?

Spring **OR** Fall?

Know Your BFF?

Would she rather...

❏ Eat green beans	OR	❏ Jelly beans?
❏ Have a bad hair day	OR	❏ Monster zit day?
❏ Go to the dance with the clueless class cutie	OR	❏ Sweet class geek?
❏ Have longer lunch periods	OR	❏ Shorter school days?
❏ Most embarrassing moment: Falling in the caf	OR	❏ Getting the wrong answer in class?
❏ Be able to fly	OR	❏ Walk through walls?
❏ Watch her fave DVD (again)	OR	❏ Go the movies?
❏ Go swimming with sharks	OR	❏ Camping with bears?
❏ Write a 10-page essay	OR	❏ Do 10 pages of math?
❏ Go bowling with a BF	OR	❏ Chill out with a BFF?
❏ Win admission to an amusement park	OR	❏ Free concert tix?
❏ Break some great news	OR	❏ Tell a funny story?
❏ Eek! Lose her bikini top	OR	❏ Surprise visit from Aunt Flo?
❏ Skim the sales	OR	❏ Save, then splurge?
❏ Get it done ASAP	OR	❏ Put it off 'til tomorrow?

Friend Fill-In
Spill it! What is her...

Most embarrassing moment _____
_____
_____

First crush _____

Favorite teacher _____

Proudest accomplishment _____

Childhood nickname _____

First concert _____

Secret talent _____

Celeb look-alike _____

Prized possession _____

Lucky charm _____

Secret crush _____

Favorite movie candy _____

Most played song _____

Can't-miss TV show _____

The 💜 of the Matter

What sits atop your bestie's priority list? Rank 'em from 1 (super important) to 5 (least important) and give yourself a point for every number you match on your bud's list.

_____ **Having a boyfriend**

_____ **Being popular**

_____ **Getting an A**

_____ **Excelling in sports**

_____ **Getting along with sibs**

_____ **Landing a dream job**

_____ **Being rich and famous**

_____ **Helping others**

_____ **Loving a pet**

_____ **Traveling the world**

_____ **Just having fun**

Now, go through the questions, with each of you revealing how you answered for one another. Give yourself a point for every right answer.

NOT MATCHING UP?

If your scores are a tad uneven or super low, don't sweat it. That doesn't mean you didn't pass the best bud test. It may just be a matter of lucky (or unlucky!) guesses, or maybe one of you pays more attention to the specific, personal details while the other is more of a big-picture pal. Either way, use this as a jumping-off point to work on getting closer and chatting more about what's on your mind. Your friendship can only get more fab!

30 POINTS OR MORE: Know-It-Alls

You're so in synch with your chica, it's spooky. Congrats on paying attention to what truly matters most to your BFF—that's what friendship is all about. It's clear you are close and communicate about everything. You're not afraid to share secrets or private thoughts. Keep it up by making sure you're there for her as much as she is for you. And consider yourself lucky: You've definitely found a soul mate in this sistah—and that's the kind of girl who only comes along once in a lifetime.

14-29 POINTS: Could Be Closer

You know your girl pretty well on the surface, but you guys are probably the type of friends who do stuff together a lot more than you heart-to-heart talk. Which is cool—but to get the very most out of your girl's company, maybe you should go a little deeper. Talk more openly to her about your feelings—then listen to hers, and offer advice when she asks for it. Developing a tighter bond this way will make the fun you have together more meaningful.

13 POINTS OR LESS: Hello, Strangers

You and your girl met…this morning? OK, you're a li'l clueless about the real her, but you can always learn! Have a good laugh together, then go back over this quiz and talk about why you answered the way you did (maybe you assumed she'd say her celeb look-alike was Taylor Swift, because of her amazing blonde hair). Then, give it some time. If you guys are really hanging out, you'll pick up more info about each other as the days go by. Share as much as you're willing to and your friendship will bloom into something beautiful.

Do You Make Friends Fast?

Whether it's the start of a new school year or you're heading off to summer camp, discover if you're sending out the right signals to potential pals—or if you need to switch up your style when it comes to forging new friendships.

You're in gym when your teacher tells you to partner up for soccer drills. Only problem? None of your friends are in the class. You...

A. Stand around until someone notices you're hangin' solo. If that doesn't happen, you'll just jump in with the closest group.

B. Tell your teacher you have to go to the bathroom—like *right now*—then duck into the locker room, ditching the drills.

C. Grab a ball and kick it toward the new girl next to you. She looks friendly, right?

 You and your BFF have been inseparable since the day you met. How'd the blessed union go down?

A. You gushed over her cute clutch, and she's been your personal stylist ever since.

B. She was the new girl and asked you to show her around school.

C. You went to the same pre-school and hit it off during arts 'n' crafts. You still have that macaroni necklace!

 In the mad dash to make it to math before the bell, you left your homework in your locker. Teacher will never give you a hall pass to get it. Of course, now she wants to go over the answers out loud. You plan to...

A. Find a seat far, far away from the front and pray your teacher won't call on you.

B. Smile at your closest neighbor and peek at her sheet—she won't mind sharing.

C. Look around in hopes that someone who *isn't* your teacher will notice you worksheet-less and let you look on.

 You had plans to meet your BFF at Shake Shack, but she's running late. How do you pass the time?

A. Grab a table and ask the waiter about specials.

B. Hop on a bar stool, order up an orange-swirl and chat with the cashier, who's your friend's older brother.

C. Linger outside with your eyes glued to the road. What color is her mom's car again?

 It's Labor Day weekend, and you're stuck at your dad's company cookout. He introduces you to his boss's son, who happens to be the shyest boy ever. What to do?

A. Go with him to grab a bite to eat. You can't talk if you're chewing, right?

B. Smile and bring up something safe, like what a bummer it is summer's over and school is starting. Even if he doesn't have much to say, at least you tried.

C. Ask him loads of get-acquainted questions, then take him to mingle with the other kids.

With school being so hectic, you've totally lost touch with your new bestie from summer day camp. How do you reconnect?

A. Shoot her an evite to your weekly Saturday sleepover with the girls. She'll love your group!

B. Wait 'til she calls you. You gave her your number, so she'll dial when she gets a minute.

C. Text her and arrange a meet-up at your fave lunch spot.

It's your b-day bash, and your parents are letting you plan a party—whatever you want. What's your scene?

A. A night of rock 'n' bowl. You'll fill the bowling alley, since you're inviting practically the entire school and all the kids you know from youth group!

B. A pizza party with your friends and a few other VIPs (like your crush and his friends, of course!).

C. A quiet dinner at your favorite Mexican joint with your fam and a couple of buds.

You and your BFF want to try out for the school musical, and auditions are tomorrow. Last minute, she gets stage fright and totally bails. You...

A. Ask if she'll at least come to support you while you give it a go.

B. Forget it. There's no way you can stand in front of those scary judges alone.

C. Tell her it's no problem and wonder if you can sing both parts in the duet you two had prepared.

Add up to reveal if you can make pals in a pinch or if you're baffled by new buds.

1.	A. 2	B. 1	C. 3
2.	A. 3	B. 2	C. 1
3.	A. 1	B. 3	C. 2
4.	A. 2	B. 3	C. 1
5.	A. 1	B. 2	C. 3
6.	A. 3	B. 1	C. 2
7.	A. 3	B. 2	C. 1
8.	A. 2	B. 1	C. 3

8-13 POINTS:

Shy Sistah

You're sweet and fun, and would make a great addition to any group o' girlies. So why are you shying away from making loads of new friends? Sometimes, your thanks-I'll-hide-in-the-shadows tendency has potential pals overlooking your fun-loving flavor. Burst that bashful bubble and step out of your comfy zone once in a while. You'll realize how accepting and welcoming most people can be. Plus, the best things in life, including new friendships, often require a leap of faith.

14-19 POINTS:
Chummy Chica

High-five! You've got a knack for making the most of every friendship opportunity. But you're also used to having peeps come to you—so you rarely make the move to initiate conversations with potential pals. You obviously already have the great qualities of a perfect pal, so take it up a notch and try mixing in instead of always checking in with the same ol' crew.

20-24 POINTS:
Social Superstar

Hey, sociable sister. You're a go-getter and don't wait around for friends to approach you or for things to happen. You love being surrounded by lots of peeps, and are most comfortable in huge social settings where you get the chance to meet-and-greet and mingle with new faces. Awkward silences? Never! Even though your friends list is overflowing, be sure to focus on those few tight buds to create close, lasting friendships.

You *try* to be nice to everyone, but sometimes the not-so-nice words just pop out. Reclaim your kindness! Find out if you're nice as pie or if your sassy side has turned a little less than sweet and could use a heapin' spoonful of heavenly sugar.

You and your best friend are on the prowl for the perfect back-to-school outfits when she points out the most adorable top. You...

A. Gush about how totally amazing it is. She'll be best dressed for sure.

B. Kick yourself for not finding it first, then ask her to help hunt something equally fab for you.

C. Tell her it's not her style—because, um, it's *so* not—then try it on yourself.

Your bestie just scarfed down a tuna sandwich with extra onions. When she asks you for a breath check, you try not to gag, then...

A. Look through your book bag to see if you've got an extra mint. She's gonna need one.

B. Tell her the coast is clear. It's only really bad once she starts talking, and you know she hates speaking up in class.

C. Make a stink face and let her know she's just wilted half the flowers in the state. Yeah, it's *that* bad.

Good Friend?

3

Your boy-crazy bud tells you she has a new crush. And guess what? He just so happens to be yours, too. You...

A. Listen to her rave over his baby blues and mention they'd be cute together. Because, actually, they would. *Sigh*...

B. Let her know you've been swooning over the guy since third grade, and jog her memory about last week's crush conversation.

C. Laugh and tell her she must be joking.

4

A new friend invited you to a fun-sounding bash, but turns out it's an awkward mix of her family and, gah, there's no one else there you know. You...

A. Snag a seat next to Gramps, who's sharing stories about his adventures on the high seas.

B. Grab some hors d'oeuvres, make nice with a few of her cousins and then call your mom for a ride after a half hour.

C. Make a face at your friend. "Why did you invite me to this?" you ask her.

5

Claire, the shy girl at school who never talks, spills tomato soup on her shirt at lunch. She looks like she's about to cry. You...

A. Walk over and hand her some napkins. Then let her know you have a shirt in your locker she can borrow.

B. Feel bad for her but stay in your seat. If she totally loses it, a lunch mom will help her. Maybe.

C. Try not to laugh, then roll your eyes to your crew. How did she manage to spill the *entire* Thermos?

You're psyched to finally run for Student Government prez when Hannah tells you she's running, too. You...

A. Wish her luck. Competition can be friendly.

B. Ignore her. You've got to start campaigning. You don't have time to worry about her negative energy.

C. Rant about her to your crew. She doesn't deserve the position nearly as much as you do. How *could* she?

Your *Glee*-obsessed BFF is auditioning for the school's musical after watching the Fleetwood Mac episode again. Problem is, her "Songbird" sounds more like a dying duck. You...

A. Tell her there are some super talented girls trying out, then encourage her to go for the drill team instead. Her dance skills are so amazing.

B. Support her 100%. She's probably good enough for a part in the chorus, so why crush her dream?

C. Ask her if she's prepared to be heartbroken. You're just being a good friend by saving her from what is going to surely be total embarrassment.

There is a new girl at your youth group whom you've never met before. She dresses kinda weird and her hair looks really tragic. You...

A. Invite her to sit with you and your friends, then take some time to get to know her and find out where she's moved here from.

B. Scoot over so there's room next to you on the couch, but don't make an extra big effort to include her in the conversation.

C. Ignore her. Yes, it's clear that she feels lost, but that's so *not* your problem.

MOSTLY A's: Sweetie

You're a good friend with a kind heart—even to those who aren't necessarily nice back. Keep up the good work! Your friends can count on you to speak words that are true, but never mean. You're like the woman in Proverbs 31: "She opens her mouth with wisdom, and the teaching of kindness is on her tongue." Even better, you back up your words with actions. Your selfless attitude is sure to catch the attention of other positive people.

MOSTLY B's: Inbetweenie

You're pretty nice...most of the time. You don't go out of your way to be mean to people, but you don't always go out of your way to be kind to them, either. Remember that God doesn't just want you to be good to your friends, he wants you to be good to everyone—even the guys who say stupid things or the girl no one talks to.

MOSTLY C's: Li'l Miss Meanie

You're one blunt chick. You have no problem letting people know how you feel—sugarcoating is not your thing. While friends may appreciate your honesty at times, it's never good to be intentionally hurtful. Ask yourself why you so often take jabs at others. Reveal your softer side, girl, and you'll see good things happening around you.

Got boys on the brain 24/7? Always thinking about the next dude? Here's how to figure out if you're too obsessed over guys or completely sane about sweeties. Answer the following questions to see if you're downright boy crazy.

What's the first thing you look for when you hop on the school bus in the morning?

A. An open spot next to a cutie, of course.

B. A friend. Nothin' like a good gab sesh to get you going in the a.m.

C. Any empty seat so you can catch a few more zzz's on the way.

Your bestie is spending the night, and the two of you are trying to decide what movie to watch. Your vote?

A. A romantic classic, like *The Notebook*. What can you say, you're a sucker for true love and tears.

B. An action-packed adventure, such as *The Hunger Games*. Gotta love the girl power!

C. Whatever she wants. You're so drained from the week that you'll zone out in front of anything.

The Sweetheart Dance is next week, and you've got high hopes. What do they entail?

A. A slow dance with your crush, of course! If he doesn't ask, you will.

Crush Crazy?

B. You can't wait to bust out some new dance moves with all your friends. Plus, you heard there'd be strawberry cupcakes!

C. Curling up with a book at home. Everybody will be at the dance, so you know you won't be disturbed.

You immediately notice the kid working the cake walk at your church's fund-raiser. What grabs your eye?

A. His beautiful eyes, amazing curly hair, perfect skin... must you go on?

B. He's wearing a T-shirt of your favorite band. You'll have to remember to talk to him later.

C. What kid? You're too busy ogling the cakes!

How would you rate your flirting skills?

A. If flirting were a school subject, you'd be the class valedictorian, natch.

B. You can turn on the charm when you want, but you wouldn't call yourself a pro or anything.

C. Flirting? The closest you've gotten to making eye contact with that honey in homeroom is when you handed him back a pen he dropped.

On a typical Friday night, you can usually be found...

A. Wherever the guys are, of course. Usually a basketball game, a party or the mall.

B. Hanging with your BFFs, doing whatever.

C. In your room flicking through Instagrams.

When you've got a crush, you think about him...

A. Non-stop. He's the center of your focus.

B. A lot. It definitely influences where you sit in the caf.
   You need to have the perfect view!

C. When you're hanging out. He's pretty cool, but you
   don't think about him all the time.

You're getting ready to hit a party you're positive your crush will also be attending when your friend calls. Her parents are splitting up and she's devastated. You...

A. Promise to console her tomorrow. You're not sure
   when you'll get to see that guy again!

B. Text your party friends to make sure they know you'll
   be there but you're running a little late. You don't
   want your crush to think you're a no-show!

C. Tell her you'll be right over. The crush can wait.

MOSTLY A's: Completely Crazy

Bananas for boys? You pretty much spend every moment thinking about guys. Yep, it's fun to get flirty with the fellas, but be careful not to neglect your friends and fam—not to mention responsibilities like school work—just 'cause you're crushing. Your friends are probably sick of the one-track convos, so if you really don't want to put a lid on it, talk to God about it instead. He'll never roll his eyes at you.

MOSTLY B's: Buds Before Boys

Sure, you have crushes. And you'd totally notice if a cute new guy showed up in school. But you're currently content to chill with your chicas and keep things casual with the boys. You like having guys as friends, but you're not dying to date. And that's totally fine! Other girls might be crush crazy, but you don't need to force the boyfriend flutters just to fit in.

MOSTLY C's: Too Busy Babe

Who's got time for guys? Between school, sports, extracurrics and everything else you've got going on, you sure don't. You may think you're too busy for boys, but don't rule them out completely. Guys can make great friends, too. Plus, the better you get to know boys now, the more savvy you'll be when a special someone does catch your eye. And even though you prefer to avoid boy drama, no need to spend all your time solo—live it up with a fun flock of friends!

How does a girl know when she's ready to go on a real date...yes, with a real-live boy? Maybe it hasn't even entered your realm of thought just yet. Or perhaps you can't get the idea of dating out of your head, but the roller-coaster ride of romance seems too risky and nerve-wracking.

Not that anyone's keeping score, but how many crushes have you had?

A. Does my latest boy-band obsession count?

B. Well, there's this guy in homeroom...

C. Tons! Can you say "boy-crazy"?

Have you ever had an official boyfriend?

A. Um, no way.

B. Yes, for about a minute.

C. Sure, and some official breakups.

Out of all your friends, how many have had a BF?

A. All of them, except you...

B. Not a single one, single being the operative word.

C. A few of your friends have had BFs.

When you imagine what it's like to be somebody's girlfriend, you imagine...

A. Writing his name on your sneakers.

B. Bragging rights ("My BF is awesome!").

C. Hand holding, silly secrets, private jokes.

When you talk to a guy, you...

A. Secretly worry that your hair looks totally weird.

B. Chat it up like he's any other friend.

C. Always make eye contact.

When you're into a guy, every time you see him...

A. You deliberately avoid his locker.

B. Your stomach does flip-flops.

C. A smile stretches across your face.

When you like a boy, he almost always...

A. Starts out as a friend.

B. Is the "it" guy in school.

C. Likes you first and then you warm up to him.

When a boy likes you, you usually...

A. Ignore him. What's the point?

B. Try to be nice even if you're not into him.

C. Give him a chance and see how it goes.

You can tell us: So how did your most recent crush come about?

A. Uh, isn't Crush an orange drink?

B. Your friends found out he liked you.

C. You met him in youth group and he seemed cool.

 Your ultimate first date would be...

A. Postponed indefinitely. Even the thought of talking to a dude makes your head totally spin.

B. A movie, so you wouldn't have to talk a lot. If you two seem to click in the ticket line and laugh at the same scenes, you'll go out for a post-date ice cream.

C. Something simple, maybe mountain biking and a brown-bag lunch.

10 Super Fun Date Ideas

1. **Hike around a lake and end with a picnic**
2. **Go to a playground and relive elementary school on the swings and slide**
3. **Attend a free art show, play or concert**
4. **Pull out the sidewalk chalk and challenge each other to a drawing duel**
5. **Go climbing on an indoor rock wall**
6. **Have a video game face-off**
7. **Go for ice cream cones**
8. **Volunteer at a homeless shelter**
9. **Hit the beach to build a sandcastle**
10. **Go to a garage sale and buy something weird**

MOSTLY A's: **Keep it on Crush**

To you, a "date" is a dried fruit your grandma puts in her oat-meal squares. You're definitely not boy-obsessed—and that's OK. You like being buds with boys (and every now and again a certain guy might catch your eye), but you're too focused on your own stuff for dude drama. Just one bit of advice: If fear is what's keeping you from hangin' with a guy you gen-uinely like, pray about it and see what unfolds.

MOSTLY B's: **Wait to Date**

Why take a cannonball-leap into the dating pool when you can dip your toe in first? You definitely like boys, no doubt about it, but you might not quite be ready to date just yet. If there's a boy you like to hang out with, why necessarily even call it "dating"? Keep the pressure low. Going out in groups rather than actual one-to-one dating can keep the jitters—and drama—at bay. Then you can decide if you want to hang with him again, taking it one group-date at a time. Snaps to you for keeping your love life at a pace that's within your own comfort zone. A word to the wise who are waiting for dating: Get to know a guy before you decide he's crush-worthy.

MOSTLY C's: **Definitely a Dater**

You definitely feel ready to embark on the adventure that is dating. The good news? In many ways, you *are* ready. You feel totally at ease around guys and have the maturity to manage the emotional responsibility that comes with going out with a guy. You're the kind of girl who can handle herself well and turn any dating disaster into a best-case scenario. Time to talk to your parents so you can get their advice before taking the plunge into the dating pool. And one other piece of dat-ing advice: Be mindful of balancing boy time with girls-only outings—your friends still love ya like a sister, so don't boot your besties aside every time another cutie comes into your world. Girl code!

Who's Your

They sit next to you in class. Hang out with you after band. Even help you with that pesky science lab. Yep, boys are constantly circling your orbit. So which one might be your true match? Test drive the contenders by taking our four mini-quizzes.

BOY #1: THE CHARMING CLASS CANDIDATE

It's Friday night, and Sam's promised you a super fun evening. That turns out to be the two of you, painting about a gazillion class prez campaign signs. Truth: Disappointed much?

A. No way—painting will be awesome! You grab a brush and support his aspirations, full-on.

B. Well, yeah, a li'l bit. But you're pretty sure Sam would do the same for you.

C. Big time. You make him promise to make it up to you with a dinner-and-DVD date next weekend.

Sam is Mr. Popularity, not to mention cute as can be. No wonder girls are constantly chatting with him. What's your vibe?

A. Totally not threatened. If he's into you, what's there to worry about?

B. Keeping your eyes open since you don't know him all that well yet.

C. Freaked. Those other girls had better back off!

3 Whenever you two hang with your gang, Sam dominates the conversation, spouting opinions and cracking jokes. Does this get on your nerves?

A. Of course not! He's just being his confident, cool self.

B. No, he's not coming on too too hard.

C. Uh, yeah. You'd like to get a word in before next year.

BOY #2: THE CUTE COMEDIAN

It's the night of the school talent show, and Jake is performing in a comedy skit in which he dresses like an old lady. The crowd loves him. Are you proud?

A. Of course! You always thought his weird grandma impressions were hilarious.

B. Not exactly proud, but you're glad all your classmates like him.

C. You're just praying no one will recognize him with that wig on.

You're trying to study for a big history test, but Jake keeps sending you hysterical selfies every three minutes. He thinks it'll ease your stress. Does it?

A. Yeah. Every time you glance at your phone you burst into giggles.

B. Sort of, but after the fifth one it's just distracting.

C. Of course not! How are you supposed to get any studying done with all those interruptions? You need an awesome grade, and endless snaps won't help.

 Jake loves hilarious YouTube vids but, uh, he's not so much into schoolwork. Can you relate?

A. Totally. You both go to school for the social scene.

B. You're not so into comics, but you don't mind that he is. You have enough brains for the both of you.

C. Not at all. And it bothers you that he barely managed to pass the big math test.

BOY #3: **THE GORGEOUS GEEK**

 On your b-day, Evan strolls up to your lunch table with his trumpet and serenades you in front of the whole caf! Love it or hate it?

A. Beyond love! He's won you—game over.

B. You appreciate the sentiment, but yikes, the whole scene is just a wee bit embarrassing.

C. You turn beet red, and seriously can't handle the humiliation.

 Evan's addicted to arachnids, beguiled by beetles, fascinated by flies. Your innermost thoughts, please.

A. Not your first choice of a hobby but, well, he's happy.

B. The crawlies creep you out. You can only deal as long as he gets buggy with it when you're not around.

C. Just the idea of holding hands after he's grasped a grasshopper makes your stomach, uh, hop.

 Your frenemy Fiona pulls you aside and informs you that if you keep dating a dork like Evan, your social stock is going to drop faster than the Dow after an oil-price hike. Your comeback?

A. You say, "Thanks for the advice, but I don't remember asking for any."

B. You toss off a quick, "Sorry, but who cares what you think?" Though you're ashamed to admit it worries you a tiny bit.

C. You force a smile and say, "Why? He's just a friend!"

BOY #4: THE SHY NEW GUY

You know Will's into you—during math class, he smiles at you like cah-razy. Still, he's so shy, you have to do all the talking. Cool with you?

A. Sure! His silent ways make him just that much more hunky and mysterious.

B. It's all right, for now. Once he warms to you, you're sure you won't be able to shut him up.

C. No. You wish he'd conjure up more than "uh-huh" to hold up his end of the conversation.

You heard Will got dumped by his GF at his old school. When you ask him about his ex, he says, "I'd rather not talk about her." How do you respond?

A. "Yeah, I don't talk about my exes either, actually."

B. "Sorry I asked—I was just curious."

C. "So why aren't you into talking about her? Are you ever going to tell me what happened?"

You're double-dating with your BFF and her boy. Will spends the whole night dissecting his sushi. Are you bothered by this behavior?

A. Nah. He doesn't weigh in on the convo much, but he's a great listener.

B. Kind of. You want your friends to know his fun side.

C. Definitely. Any guy who digs you has to be able to keep up with your besties, too.

SCORING: Give yourself three points for every A, two points for every B, and one point for every C. Then tally up your points to see which bachelor scored the highest! *(Got a tie? You lucky girl! Two of these guys are perf for you!)*

IF YOU PICKED

the charming class candidate...

Congrats, girl! You've got enough of your own good stuff going on that one day you'll be happy to share the spotlight with a guy. You can be proud of his accomplishments and won't get jealous when you have to share his time. Just be sure that your guy gives you the same amount of support back. If the props-giving and understanding is equal, he's a keeper.

IF YOU PICKED

the cute comedian...

You're bound to have a great time with this guy who puts the fun in funny! Keep an eye out for boys with a talent for making others (especially you) laugh. Spend time with someone like this and you'll realize the benefit of not taking life too seriously. Just make sure he's able to keep a straight face every once in a while. You'll want to have some down-to-earth conversations from time to time, too.

IF YOU PICKED

the gorgeous geek...

What a smarty. You're the kind of gal that can appreciate a good guy for all the right reasons. This boy is the perfect package: Intelligent, considerate and interesting. What's more, you couldn't give a flying furball what other (mean) people think about your choice of crushes. You know that a person's true fabulousness is all about what's going on inside.

IF YOU PICKED

the shy new guy...

Your work's cut out for you, but it could be worth it. He's probably worried about making the wrong moves (hence the antisocial antics). So be patient. Yep, you'll do most of the talking, and yep, it'll be tough getting him to reveal his feelings. But if he's the right guy for you, he'll gradually let down his guard. You'll build up trust, which will stick you together like Krazy Glue.

Faith and Family

We know faith and family are super important to you, but do you always show just how much you love 'em? These quizzes reveal what kind of sis and daughter you are (hint: we know it's an amazing one).

How Close R You

A tight bond with Mom is totally worth the work. So grab two pens and some paper, and ask Mom (or your stepmom or your aunt) to join you. Read the questions together but answer them privately—no peeking! When you're done, compare your papers. It'll kick off some ultra-revealing conversations.

Uh-oh. You're running late again. When Mom grounds you for missing curfew, it's 'cause...

A. She thinks you go out too much and wants you home more. When did you last spend a weekend together?

B. Um, how else are you going to learn to meet deadlines and be responsible?

C. Hello! Anytime you're not in right on the dot, she's sure every siren is an ambulance hauling you to the emergency room.

D. Ground you? For what? Her philosophy is, "Better late than never."

Your mom would def make the final round on which reality show:

A. *American Idol*

B. *Food Network Star*

C. *So You Think You Can Dance*

D. *Survivor*

3 It seems like there's always some kind of election happening. Your mom is registered to vote, right?

A. Of course, as a Republican.

B. Yep, she's proud to be a Democrat.

C. Oh, I think she's an Independent.

D. Er, no, she isn't registered.

4 When your mom was a girl, what did she most want to be when she grew up?

A. A mom! Duh.

B. A teacher

C. President of the United States

D. A rock star!

5 Which famous woman would your mom like to meet?

A. A tech guru like Marissa Mayer

B. Oprah, the total media genius

C. Rachael Ray, the most fun cook ever

D. A First Lady like Michelle Obama

6 Dream trip! Where would your mom go?

A. Anywhere that requires her to pack the SPF.

B. A hiking or biking adventure tour.

C. A grand Mediterranean cruise.

D. Camping in a state park where the entire fam would have a blast.

Which classic movie does your mom love?

7

A. *Groundhog Day*

B. *Titanic*

C. *Ferris Bueller's Day Off*

D. *Back to the Future*

When your mom was a teen, what was her style?

8

A. Preppy: khakis, pleated skirts, button-down shirts, polos, sweater vests and headbands

B. Deadhead: faded jeans, halter tops, tie-dyed tees, beaded jewelry and patchouli

C. '80s chic: tiered skirts, ripped fishnets, fingerless gloves, hair scrunchies and smudged eyeliner

D. Casual: jeans, concert tees, and Jack Purcells in almost every color of the rainbow

If your mother's BFF were to tell her something and swear her to secrecy, your mom would...

9

A. Take it to her grave. When someone says zip those lips, she really listens. You'd never have to worry about your little brother telling the whole school who you are crushing on.

B. Only tell a few people she's sure would keep it under wraps. She isn't a gossip, but everyone is human!

C. Spill. She means well, but she's not one to keep things all bottled up. She wouldn't post it on Facebook or anything....

D. Just tell your father (or significant other). She's pretty much a vault and everyone trusts her, but your dad didn't seem overly shocked when you asked him to pick up some pads at the drugstore.

All of them are important, but which quality does your mom think matters most in a guy?

A. Ambition. She likes a guy who's driven, industrious and goal-oriented.

B. Kindness. No "bad boy" personas (and don't even get her started on dudes who get in trouble).

C. Honesty. A relationship is nada without trust.

D. Respect. She likes to see that sparkle in his eye, and know that his values are true blue.

BONUS ROUND

1. Did your mom wear braces?
2. What subject did she rock in school?
3. Does she believe in love at first sight?
4. What's her greatest accomplishment so far (besides you, of course)?
5. What's her signature scent?
6. How old was she when she got her period?
7. Which president was in office the day she was born?
8. What year did she graduate high school?
9. Would your mom fly to outer space if she had the chance?
10. Did she wear glasses as a kid?

15-20 POINTS: **Totally Tight**

Have you been reading Mom's journal? You know her sooo well. That's great—your mom clearly shares a lot with you and hopefully you do the same. Even if you scored 100%—pretty unlikely but still—use this quiz to have some fun together. *Ferris Bueller* is her favorite flick? Rent it this weekend and have a movie momfest (don't forget the popcorn). Her style as a teen was casual? See if she still has any of those vintage T-shirts stashed away, then try a few spritzes of her signature scent.

8-14 POINTS: **Cozy Close**

We have a feeling this is where most girls land on the mom scale. You know her well enough, but you probably just learned a few of her best-kept secrets. Awesome. Use this quiz to kick open the doors of communication even wider—bringing you and your mom closer. Chat more in-depth and ask her why she values ambition or honesty or whatever topic comes up (hey, why not even have a real political discussion?). Curious about her younger years? Flip through one of Mom's old yearbooks to get to know what she was like way back when.

1-7 POINTS: **Distant Daughter**

You two could wear "Hello, my name is…" tags. Sure, you adore each other but get to know Mom on a deeper level. If you're both busy and in your own worlds, make an effort to have some mother-daughter bonding time. Even if it's over carryout pizza at the kitchen table, don't eat in silence. Ask your mom to tell you what issues were important to her when she was your age. Find out why she loved science and hated phys ed. Listen to her fave music, and maybe even catch a concert together. Bottom line? It's never too late to get tight with Mom.

Are You Good at Being Grateful?

Sure, you're thankful for all the sweet things your friends and fam do for you. But how good are you at actually expressing appreciation? Find out here if you're giving off good gratitude vibes—or if you could do a better job of counting your blessings.

1. You're at a family brunch, and Grandma presents you a sweater she knitted by hand. Too bad it's a hideous puke-brown and super itchy. How do you show her props?

A. Put it on. It's ugly and majorly uncomfortable, but Grams made it with love!

B. Say a quick "thank you" with a sweet smile, then ask her to pass the OJ.

C. Um, you don't. You don't want to lie to the lady, so why act all phony?

♡ THANK ❀ YOU

Your BFF gave up a trip to the mall with her mom to tutor you for a major Spanish test. How will you make it up to her?

A. Whip up a dozen of her favorite double-fudge cake pops with sprinkles.

B. Give her a hug the next day at school.

C. Quickly mention that you'd return the favor, but tutoring is so not your thing.

You got tonsa awesome gifts from your friends at your birthday blow-out. When did you pop your thank-you notes in the mail?

A. The morning after the party, of course.

B. Within two weeks. You got a little busy 'cause school got crazy.

C. Thank-you notes? What thank-you notes?

Snow day! And—ugh—it's your turn to shovel the drive-way. But when you bundle up and head outside, your next-door neighbor is doing the job for you. What do you say to him?

A. "That's sooo sweet!" Then run inside and make him a huge thermos of hot cocoa.

B. "Thanks, but you really didn't have to do that. I'll do your driveway during the next snow, deal?"

C. "Hey, way to double up on the driveways!" Then you point out some spots he's missed.

It's time to swap Christmas prezzies with your BFF. She gets you a beautiful necklace with a tiny silver heart. And you got her...a monkey keychain. How do you deal?

A. Beg for a three-month advance on your allowance, motor to the mall and trade that keychain in for a necklace and bracelet.

B. Accept happily, then write her a totally sweet letter telling her how much you appreciate her.

C. Keep the keychain, then pocket the pendant. Her parents buy her so much stuff anyway. She won't exactly notice if you skip a gift this year.

Dad's finally painting your room a rockin' red, but he only gets one wall done before bolting to handle a work crisis. He says he'll finish next week, so 'til then, you'll be stuck with the wacky walls. Your feelings?

A. You'll just finish the job yourself, even though it would have been a great dad-daughter endeavor.

B. You totally understand and wait it out until he's able to break out the brush again.

C. You're disappointed and dump your feelings on Dad any chance you get.

Your BFF has supported you from the sidelines at every single swim competition. Now it's her turn to shine in an orchestra recital...which so happens to be the same night as your big meet. What do you do?

A. Tell your coach you can't compete. She's been there for you, so you can't just bail on her stage debut.

B. Be sure she knows you'll be there in spirit, but that you can't miss a meet. Then scoot to her house as soon as you can for a play-by-play of the show.

C. Shoot her a quick text explaining that swimming is way cooler than saxophone, then wish her luck at the concert. She'll know you're just kidding around...

While you're at school, your mom completely cleans and organizes your bedroom. What's your reaction?

A. You give her a hug and let her know how much it means to you—even though you're actually a little peeved she spent the day going through your stuff.

B. You tell her it looks great, but that next time you'll gladly clean your room by yourself.

C. You can't quite hide how annoyed you are. Not only did she invade your privacy, but now you're never going to be able to find anything she put away. Ugh!

MOSTLY A's:
Overly Obliged

You're so grateful for any kindness someone shows you, you're bascially willing to do backflips for 'em. Which is all well and good, but remember there's no need to be over the top. Going overboard can actually have the opposite effect (as in you can come off as fake, which is just so not the point). Skip the showy sentiments and go for a simple thank you spoken from the heart. That's more than enough to show your appreciation to the people who are truly important to you. But don't be worried about it, because you're totally on the right track.

MOSTLY B's:
Grateful Girl

You're right on the money when it comes to showing others just how much their generosity means to you. Not only are you great at expressing your feelings, you know that thoughful etiquette stuff (like sending a timely thank-you note) isn't a stuffy custom—it's a move that really says, "You mean something to me, and I'm taking the time to let you know it." Your people skills are rare and amazing, so keep giving back just the way you do now. Then watch others give the same snaps to you!

MOSTLY C's:
Slightly Thankless

Sounds like someone needs to fine-tune their thank-yous. We're not saying you have to force amazement every time someone does something nice for you, but try to show some love here and there. Otherwise, your attitude can come off unappreciative or indifferent—and potentially hurt other people. So practice saying a heartfelt thanks for even the tiniest things—when your little sis picks up your plate after dinner; when your neighbor gives you a lift home from school. Whatever it takes to let that warm, fuzzy, caring chick you really are shine through!

You love your siblings, but it's not always easy to be part of a family, especially when you have a li'l sis messing with your stuff or your big bro bossing you around. Since you can't hibernate in your bedroom by yourself all the time, find out how well you handle the familial heat, sis.

1 Your little brother is struggling with the same science project that gave you grief two years ago. When he bursts into major waterworks, you...

A. Pat him on the back and say, "Yeah, good luck with that." Then, you go back to texting with your BFF.

B. Put in your earbuds. You hate hearing his bratty cry.

C. See if you can give him a couple of quick pointers. It's all coming back to you...

2 Your sister is hogging the TV—again—and your favorite show is on. How do you deal?

A. Dance wildly in front of the screen until she gets so annoyed, she leaves the room.

B. Grab the remote and change the channel. She can watch in your parents' room.

C. Ask if she wants to watch your show with you. She might be willing to change the channel if she has company. Plus, you think she'll love it, if she gives it a half a chance.

Sister Are You?

3

You're on a road trip with the fam, and your brother won't stop kicking your seat. What do you do?

A. Whip around and get him square between the eyes with a squirt gun. You brought it for exactly this kind of occasion. He's always pestering you in some way.

B. Shoot him a look, then recline your seat back all the way to cram him.

C. Ask him to stop, then see if he wants to play a travel game with you.

4

You and your BFF are in your room poring over the recently released school yearbook when your super annoying little sister barges in wanting a peek. You…

A. Tell her to have a look, then yell, "Time's up!" as you snatch it away in less than a second.

B. Yell for your dad to make her go away. She doesn't know anyone in your yearbook, anyway.

C. Promise you'll show her later and give her the scoop on the teachers she'll have when she's in your grade. You didn't have anyone guiding you, but why keep her in the dark?

5

You and your fam are going on vacay and staying in your grandma's tiny condo for a week. You excited?

A. For the trip? Yes! You just hope you and your older sister don't kill each other before it's over.

B. Of course. Three words: Pool. All. Day.

C. Yeah! Maybe your big brother will even take you mountain biking.

6 It's your brother's birthday—he just turned 16. What do you do?

A. Make him a birthday cake...for smashing in his face—it'll be hilarious!

B. Eat as much of his ice-cream cake as you can before his dorky friends dig in. You'll give him a card (and maybe a gift) after the party's over. No need to make a big deal of it.

C. Buy him a cool keychain. He'll finally have his driver's license, and he's promised to cart ya places.

7 Your little sis had a solo in the Sunday school pageant, but she flubbed a line. What do you say to her when the show is over?

A. "At least you weren't accompanying yourself on piano—you probably would've screwed that up, too."

B. You weren't there, thank goodness. You bailed to go hang out at a friend's house.

C. "Your singing is beautiful! I like how you made the song uniquely yours."

MOSTLY A's: Sassy Sister

When it comes to siblings, you're not exactly pouring on the syrupy sweetness. When it comes to getting along, it's your way or the highway—you're really not all that interested in going out of your way to accommodate them. We totally get that having sibs around can be pesky—but have you ever considered that perhaps you're part of the problem? Maybe your big sister started it or your little brother won't leave you alone, but there's nothing stopping you from resetting the tone. Those sibs just might take a cue or two from you and try to be kinder, too. Believe it or not, it's possible to make peace with your siblings.

MOSTLY B's: Closed-off Chica

You're not necessarily mean to your sibs, but you're not exactly friendly, either. Generally, you just pretend they're invisible. You'd rather ignore annoying brothers and sisters than have to deal with them. It's totally normal for siblings to get on your nerves sometimes, but try giving them some of your attention once in a while. You'll probably discover they're not as lame as you thought. The better you get along, the less stressful your family life will be. Hey, you all have to live together, so make the best of it!

MOSTLY C's: Family Friend

You've got your siblings' backs and, chances are, they've got yours. Sure, sometimes they're super annoying—but you make it work. You try to be patient and kind and supportive. After all, you can't just make a swap for a new family if you don't like the one you've got—yeah, you're stuck with them and you love it.

Got Spiritua

Sometimes, staying firmly grounded in faith feels natural and reassuring. But other times? Complicated questions come up about God, church and the Bible, and it's enough to make your head start spinning. How do you handle all the tricky toughies that come up?

How often do you ponder the big questions about spirituality and God and all that?

A. All the time. It seems like you're always questioning God and, sometimes, even your faith.

B. Often. Even though it's pretty random, you wonder about these things regularly.

C. Sometimes. Certain events, like funerals, cause questions to pop up in your mind.

D. You rarely, if ever, even think about this stuff.

What questions spin around in your brain the most?

A. Who—or what!—is God? Is he really listening?

B. What's up with all the different religions? Which belief system is right?

C. Why does God allow bad stuff to happen? Why do bad things happen to good people?

D. What's the purpose of life? If there is a God, does he even care? You've got a lot of big questions.

How do you feel when you have questions about your spiritual or religious beliefs?

A. Unhappy. You don't like to doubt God.

B. Worried that your faith isn't rock-solid enough.

C. Intrigued. There's so much to learn about God—and you love a good mystery.

D. Unfazed. You're sure God will use your questions to somehow help you grow in understanding.

Sometimes, you just can't get certain questions out of your head. How do you figure it all out?

A. The Bible says to believe, so you hold to that belief.

B. You go online looking for answers.

C. You break out your Bible and pray.

D. You get your parents and friends engaged in some deep convos.

How do you think your friends and family might respond to some of your faith questions?

A. You get a little worried they'll assume you don't have enough faith in God.

B. Your peeps are open-minded, so you can always find someone willing to banter.

C. You don't know anyone who would have a clue about God's truth. You sometimes feel alone in your beliefs.

D. You don't like talking about your faith. It's kind of a personal thing.

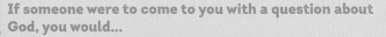

If someone were to come to you with a question about God, you would...

A. Be a little freaked that you might give the wrong answer. You're not exactly an expert.

B. Talk openly and honestly about your beliefs.

C. Listen. No guarantees, but maybe you'll get insights from each other.

D. Tell her to talk to a pastor or someone who knows more about the whole faith thing.

Question No. 1 and No. 2

If you answered A, B, C or D: There's no right or wrong answer here. God wants you to ask questions so he can lead you to what's true in life's grand game of Truth or Dare. Even doubt is a normal part of the process when it comes to understanding the truth of God's existence, and it's a solemn promise that God is not threatened by it. A good place to start? Job, Ecclesiastes and the Psalms are filled with details about God and his work in the world. Way better than a fortune cookie!

Question No. 3

If you answered A or B: Know that just about everyone goes through times of doubt and uncertainty. Questions and crises help you grow in faith and deepen your comprehension of it. Don't let flaky feelings stand in the way of exploring your faith. Forge on!

If you answered C or D: You are willing and even excited about delving into tough questions, which will help strengthen your walk. If you do slip into doubt or fear, know that it's perfectly OK to feel like you're on shaky ground at times. Just don't stay stuck there!

Question No. 4

If you answered A, B, C or D: These are all good places to get answers, even better if combined. Talk with others about what you read in the Bible. Beef up your faith facts with some research. Remember that not everything you read online is true. Measure what others say and what you read against the Bible. God always provides answers to the questions you ask—all you have to do is pay close attention.

Question No. 5

If you answered A, C or D: Don't let your fears of what others might think stand in the way of seeking answers. If you don't know a youth leader, pastor or group of friends with whom you can share your heart, pray that God will lead you to a better understanding. He's always listening.

If you answered B: Awesome that you can talk openly with friends who are rooted in their faith—enjoy these gab sessions with your BFFs. Don't necessarily agree on certain points? Show respect as you help each other explore all the adventures faith brings.

Question No. 6:

If you answered A, B or C: When a friend comes to you with questions, it means she trusts you enough to share what's in her heart (and, psst, no one expects you to have all the answers when it comes to faith). Bouncing ideas and insights off of each other can be a great way to build bonds, too.

If you answered D: Taking your friend to hash out questions with a pastor is a great option—and will probably help you too!—but don't discount your own ability to hear her out and provide insights. You probably have more knowledge than ya think.

PETS
Mini Quiz!

1. How many pets do you have?

2. What kind of pets do you have? And what are their names?

3. Which one is your favorite?

4. What is the cutest thing one of them has ever done?

5. What is the worst thing one of them has ever done?

6. Do you think you could live without your animals?

7. Are there any pets you want now but don't/can't have yet?

Every girl's different. So it makes sense every girl connects to God differently, too, right? Discover how you connect best— and you just might realize it's easier to dial up God than you thought.

You like learning more about faith because...

A. You always hit it off with other girls who are strong in their faith. Birds of a feather, as they say...

B. It gets you closer and closer to feeling God's presence. And that happens to be pretty amazing.

C. It's all about spreading the love!

D. Your family has so many cool faith-based traditions.

When someone asks you to a church event, before you commit you first want to know...

A. Who in your crew is gonna be there.

B. If there will be some down time for quiet prayer and devotions. You love to go deep into your faith.

C. How you being there might help someone else.

D. What else might be on the family calendar—ya gotta be sure you aren't double-booking.

You absorb a lot more at a Bible study if...

A. You have lots of time for a group discussion.

B. The group leader passes out great stuff to read and think about.

C. It focuses on ways to make a real difference in the world. You're pretty practical that way.

D. You do a quick review with your parents at dinner.

4 **You'd be interested in going on a church trip if it...**

A. Involves other girls your age.

B. Gives you the chance to meditate in a new environment. Checking out holy spaces is important to you.

C. Genuinely serves a cause you care about.

D. Is the same trip your older sis did.

5 **You think of prayer as a way to...**

A. Give praise to God as a group.

B. Connect one-on-one with God.

C. Partner with God in changing the world.

D. Do something that is what, well, everyone in your fam does.

6 **When it comes to sharing your beliefs...**

A. You and your friends are definitely like-minded.

B. You're tight with God, but that's your personal biz.

C. You use your God-given talents, such as art or storytelling, as a way to help others.

D. You usually keep it in the family.

Mostly A's: **Social Spirit**

You prefer to connect to your faith through friendship with others. You're an outgoing girl with a great big heart. And you're in luck—because relationships are an important part of being Christian. Friends challenge, encourage and keep us accountable for our actions. Your fun and friendly personality can attract others to God. Your commitment to God is solid, even if some of your pals don't understand God's love quite the way you do.

Mostly B's: **Private Passion**

You prefer focusing on your one-on-one relationship with God, and that's cool. Your faith is private and personal—it's important everyone understands their individual connection to God from within. But that never means you should always go it alone. You might be missing out on the important element of knowing God's love in relationship with others—and you can bet there are countless precious lessons about God's principles in those shared experiences. So consider joining youth group, and make some awesome new friends!

Mostly C's: Giving Heart

You understand what it means to be God's vessel of love. You use your faith to make a whopping difference in the world. You engage with God by being in service, getting involved in activities that can shift and uplift. Volunteering is probably important to you, and you're a natural at planning fund-raisers for worthy charitable causes. That's good news! God can use you in a mighty way to spread his love. Just remember that overload can easily lead to burnout. Balance your pro-active ways with personal moments of silent stillness so he can renew your energies.

Mostly D's: Foundation of Faith

Religious tradition and church events must be influential parts of your life. Your ties to your family heritage are at the root of who you are spiritually. But be careful that your relationship with God isn't always on cruise control. It's great to have solid faith-based roots, but at some point you need to use your family tradition merely as a launching pad for your own faith journey. Godspeed.